Praise for *The New American High School*

"Once again, Ted Sizer has written a book that will wake us up—he reminds us about the power of good questions and how that can spark a child's interest to pursue many diverse fields and to learn in multiple ways that might surprise both the child and the teacher. I will hold it close and hear Ted's beautiful voice reminding us that our work is worthy and urging us on to make teaching and learning better and better for all children, teachers, and communities."

—Linda Nathan, founding headmaster, Boston Arts Academy, and executive director of the Center of Art in Education at Boston Arts Academy

"Ted Sizer distills a lifetime of listening into this volume. Prodding us, as he did in life, not toward a single answer but toward our most thoughtful questions and toward the schools our children deserve."

—Kath Connolly, director of partnerships, The Learning Community, Rhode Island

"In this, his final treatise on the promise for American secondary education, Ted Sizer masterfully weaves his own personal narrative with a call to educators to take a hatchet to the lingering dysfunctions of schools, much as his own mother incited him to prepare the turkeys one Thanksgiving when he was a young boy. With a tenor of profound urgency, Sizer's voice is as prescient and clear today as when we first met nearly a quarter of a century ago."

—Jed Lippard, head of school, Prospect Hill Academy Charter School, Massachusetts

ALSO BY THEODORE R. SIZER

Secondary Schools at the Turn of the Century

Places for Learning, Places for Joy:
Speculations on American School Reform

Horace's Compromise:
The Dilemma of the American High School

Horace's School:
Redesigning the American High School

Horace's Hope:
What Works for the American High School

The Students Are Watching:
Schools and the Moral Contract (with Nancy Faust Sizer)

Keeping School:
Letters to Families from Principals of Two Small Schools
(with Deborah Meier and Nancy Faust Sizer)

The Red Pencil:
Convictions from Experience in Education

THE
NEW AMERICAN
HIGH SCHOOL

Theodore R. Sizer

FOREWORD BY
DEBORAH MEIER

INTRODUCTION BY
NANCY FAUST SIZER

JB JOSSEY-BASS
A Wiley Brand

Published by Jossey-Bass

A Wiley Brand

One Montgomery Street, Suite 1200, San Francisco, CA 94104-4594—
www.josseybass.com

Jossey-Bass books and products are available through most bookstores. To contact Jossey-Bass directly call our Customer Care Department within the U.S. at 800-956-7739, outside the U.S. at 317-572-3986, or fax 317-572-4002.

Wiley publishes in a variety of print and electronic formats and by print-on-demand. Some material included with standard print versions of this book may not be included in e-books or in print-on-demand. If this book refers to media such as a CD or DVD that is not included in the version you purchased, you may download this material at **http://booksupport.wiley.com**. For more information about Wiley products, visit **www.wiley.com**.

Library of Congress Cataloging-in-Publication Data has been applied for and is on file with the Library of Congress.
ISBN 978-1-118-52642-2 (cloth); ISBN 978-1-118-58498-9 (ebk.);
ISBN 978-1-118-58497-2 (ebk.); ISBN 978-1-118-58482-8 (ebk.)

Printed in the United States of America
FIRST EDITION

HB Printing   10 9 8 7 6 5 4 3 2 1

CONTENTS

FOREWORD BY DEBORAH MEIER

*I*n every page of the book that follows, I hear the voice and heart of Ted Sizer. His way of thinking and of making sense of the world of schooling, which had such a deep impact on my life, comes through in these important pages.

. . .

In 1983, I was being pressed by former students and families to think about extending the work of the Central Park East elementary schools in East Harlem into secondary school. Our work in New York City began in the early 1970s in East Harlem, during the alternative high school movement. The general lament: "We're doing okay in regular middle schools and high schools, *but* . . . we've rarely had a serious intellectually challenging or interesting experience in school since we left sixth grade." In short: why not?

Reason one: I was a kindergarten teacher with strong views—even about secondary education—but inexperienced in educating students older than twelve, and very nervous about thirteen- and fourteen-year-olds in groups of more than two!

Reason two: I disliked the tightly prescribed Regents curriculum that New York State's high schools had to conform to, especially if we were going to be working with students who did not easily take to standardized testing and a fast but narrow scanning of subject matter.

Reason three: the course requirements for a diploma were a distraction when one was thinking about an intellectually serious secondary school.

Reasons two and three were especially problematic for those of us who were running progressive schools. I knew the state's requirements were not good for anyone, and my own three children's secondary school experiences reminded me of this daily. But experience also told me that foolish requirements made less difference for young people with lots of family-supported extracurricular intellectual and artistic resources than it did for the young people of East Harlem. The Regents tests are incredibly sensitive to what we lately call "social capital." If we were going to explore progressive education on a secondary school level for students who didn't come to us with all that social capital, it would have to be radically different than anything I was aware of in the public or private sector. I wanted something even better than (but similar to) the independent school I had attended. Luckily I had gone to a grade 7–12 school that I admired (Fieldston) and that I thought was almost good enough for the children who went to our elementary schools. But it seemed unlikely that I could get the support and freedom to translate that kind of education into New York's public system, city or state, much less the even more transformative example of Fieldston. (I'd also have to hurry and get a New York State–approved high school principal's license.)

• • •

Then in the early 1980s, I read an essay by Ted Sizer, which became part of his forthcoming book, *Horace's Compromise*. And my life changed.

Here was a man whose history was so different from my own—educationally, personally, and professionally—yet who had reached more or less the same conclusions, and moreover had taken his experience to new depths and details. If only I could carry out some of these ideas, I thought . . . Well, at first I thought mostly of his prestige and how that might help us convince the Authorities. A former Harvard dean of education ("boy wonder" and all that), an academic and author, a former principal of one of the most prestigious private prep schools, a New England WASP—and comfortable among the rich and powerful. That's how I thought of him. But all that turned out to be the least of it.

And when I cleverly sent a message via Courtney Cazden at Harvard, who had worked with Ted when he was dean, Ted did what I later understood to be the predictable thing, knowing him as I do now. He said, "Great. Tell her to call me." I did, and he answered the phone in that warm and welcoming voice.

And so began more than a quarter century of closely following his work and his ideas. These ideas became flesh-and-blood schools, starting with Central Park East Secondary School (CPESS). We were able to convince all the key players, and above all the state commissioner, Tom Sobel, to allow us to waive counting course credits as a requirement for graduation and to waive any existing or forthcoming Regents exams. Sobel said, "Don't worry; I'll be there for your first graduating class, and I'll hand them all diplomas."

(A commitment he carried out some years later when our first class graduated and when he signed a written agreement that has outlasted his tenure—and is still in effect twenty-five years later. He was a critical protector of some of the most successful innovators still thriving in the state, and maybe the nation.)

Sobel's bold step was not primarily based on his knowledge of my work, but rather on his knowledge of Ted's. With his support came the support of New York City's chancellor—who met with Ted (as did all subsequent chancellors—who changed often in those days). There were also meetings with the mayor, the local school board, and the United Federation of Teachers.

We seized the moment and ran with it. We pulled together a basic plan, moved Central Park East (CPE) elementary school and the yet-to-be-created CPESS into a new building, and started recruiting staff and students. The school, we decided, would be small (maximum 450 students, grades 7–12) and would operate in three "stages," mostly based on the students' ages. Like my old high school—with its Forms I, II, and III—we had Divisions 1, 2, and 3. We decided to make each division multiage—continuing an elementary school practice in place at CPE—and to create two interdisciplinary subjects: the humanities and math/science. All students in the first two divisions were provided with the same program. It was only in Division 3, which we called the Senior Institute, that we considered holding kids for an extra year. It was when students reached age sixteen that school was organized explicitly to prepare them for the transition to "the world"—by showing the world (by presenting their work to a small sample of that world) that the students could do the work expected of smart seventeen- to nineteen-year-olds—while also designing a plan for their post-CPESS lives. We hoped to bring Ted's plan into a real-live public "inner-city" school. And we did.

The first things we did when we started CPESS was to design a basic structure. Ted had told us, "Keep the structure simple so that you can attend to the complexity of each student's mind and of the subject matter you are studying." That was the motto I kept in mind. Whenever I ran into a dilemma, I tried to choose the simplest solution and the one that kept the power close to the mutual ground we shared with students and their families.

Then we—the original seven teachers—asked ourselves what would it be that students would have to demonstrate to "us" before they received our diploma, and who would be the "us"—the judges. We sat there and tried to think of what it might mean to use our minds well—which was number one of the then nine principles. Keep it simple, Ted urged again.

We first tried listing all the things we thought every graduate should know and be able to do (that was the common language of the day) in each of our disciplinary fields. We filled every blackboard in the room in tiny print. That got us nowhere. Because once we printed it all up, everyone realized that at best we could ourselves meet only the goals in our own field—if that.

So we tried to explore the issue another way: What qualities of mind are common across all subject matter, all disciplines? What unites us intellectually? As we developed our answers to this question, we knew we were becoming clearer about the significance of the habits we came up with and our idea that the primary function of public education was to nourish and nurture the habits needed for a strong democratic culture.

At CPESS, we settled on five "habits of mind" that crossed all disciplines. Then began the never-ending task of asking ourselves how we might go about making them accessible to all our students, and how we would judge our own and our student's work along the way through the three divisions in about six years and, finally, as the basis for sending them across the stage with a diploma. It took hours and hours, of course, and over the first two years—while our new students were completing grades 7 and 8—we had the luxury of working carefully to see that there was continuity between what and how we taught in grades 7 through 10 and what was expected of our graduates at the end of "grade 12"—or whenever a student was "ready."

• • •

In those first heady days in 1983–1985, we were a small gang of maybe seven or eight schools. Ted's hope was that we'd grow to perhaps fifteen schools nationwide—schools of all types in terms of student population, governance, and so on. He was responding to the challenge so often made to his ideas: that they were utopian. We would, he believed, learn from the experiences of this small, nationwide coalition of schools what stumbling blocks we would need to overcome as well as the unexpected successes we might uncover. We would work closely together and with him. Our network included a private school in the southwest, a Catholic school in the northeast, and several "regular" public schools—from the wealthiest suburban to the poorest rural—with unusual leaders in communities that were prepared to support them.

A similar process went on at one after another of the schools that joined the Coalition. Ted's running commentary on our work was the steady force behind the accomplishments of the founding schools, and of others that engaged in his reforms. Fortunately, both in his books and speeches and in personal conversation, Ted told stories that helped us think these issues through—and pointed to readings that might deepen our conversations. We met annually at Brown University, told each other stories, and visited each other's schools. Ted reminded us that the most important part of our work was in changing the nature of the conversation in schools and in the larger world.

That was his goal, and in its simplicity it was, of course, grandiose and complex.

And through his efforts, the Coalition started a magazine—*Horace*. The original editor, Kathleen Cushman, filled each issue with accounts from the field, sharing successful and unsuccessful attempts to embody the principles despite all the constraints that come with operating in reality.

In the next decades, many other schools joined our ranks; we created regions so that the schools could work more easily with each other throughout the year, but got together nationally for an annual convention whose principal presenters were the educators in our schools. Under this national umbrella, many of our New York State and other Coalition sister schools took different paths, spurning the idea of a "model" because of Ted's—and our own—respect for our individual communities, but agreeing about the same set of values.

• • •

I held my breath for a while: would Ted turn out to have feet of clay? It never happened. What struck me as unusual from day one was his unequivocal sympathy for the many people he encountered during his study of American high schools that led to *Horace's Compromise*, an unusually teacher- and student-friendly book that had made me cautiously prepared to trust him. I had developed a decidedly skeptical mind-set about "academics," but Ted belonged to that "other" category. He acknowledged their best intentions and struggled with them to imagine a different set of "compromises" that would work better for young and old alike. It was not compromises per se that he opposed, but making the wrong ones. Horace was not the villain of his piece, nor an unusual hero; rather, he was an English teacher trying his hardest to find ways to use his time and his mind to help his 130 to 150 students—a different group every semester—learn to be strong readers and writers. Ted's book demonstrated respect for the "old-fashioned" academic virtues, even as he noted that one of the most intellectually stimulating classes he observed was a shop class.

We tried our best to follow in that spirit—not condemning our less fortunate colleagues, but doing our best to be allies in their perhaps more modest efforts at reform as well.

It struck me that Ted was approaching secondary school-ing with the same mind-set that I had approached kindergar-ten and then elementary school. His high school dream was not so different than what I believed in for five-year-olds—to be known well, to be engaged with interesting materials and ideas in a setting of mutual respect. Poverty and racism com-plicate our tasks; they place some constraints on everyone involved. But we all agreed that the kind of education we offer the wealthy and talented is what we need to offer all young people. The less powerful need it even more than the already powerful. Of course, context matters, but what we sought through the Coalition of Essential Schools was a way to reach all children with the priorities, values, and intellectual stimu-lation that we witnessed in the best of private, independent schools. Only more so. And we hoped to do it without prese-lecting the most promising students or spending much more money per student than other neighboring public schools had access to.

The creation of the Coalition in the early 1980s was a criti-cal step. We weren't alone: we were part of a movement. Ted's nine principles, which were put together after many conversa-tions with good teachers, were unique and powerful. They represented not a recipe or model but a mind-set, principles that could be adapted to particular passions and particular situations. They almost seemed to be common sense, and we found few who disagreed with them, but many who thought they could not survive in the public sector.

For some of those whom I soon encountered, these prin-ciples were frustrating. "What does he mean by 'using his or her mind well'?" they complained. "Why doesn't he spell it out? What does he mean by 'decency' or faculty autonomy?" For others, the respect for the context that each educator faces was the beauty of the Coalition framework. Ted was challenging us to have our own collective dreams, not to adopt his. And he welcomed many interpretations and thus widely. variant models.

Ted went visiting often, at one school after another—probing, questioning, and always appreciating. His probes were sometimes quietly painful, but, more important, they were clearly the result of genuine curiosity and respect. They weren't "test questions" but honest probes for himself and for us. There was never a "gotcha," even when he was sometimes worried about our decisions. He figured that he was learning along with us. But from the start to the end, Ted's comments almost always came only after a lot of listening and observing. That was his hallmark: through his own behaviors, he reminded us that teaching requires knowing each child well.

By the early 1990s, Ted helped others form local support groups, such as the Center for Collaborative Education (CCE) in Boston. The launch of pilot schools as part of Boston's public system was a dream come true—and we jumped on it. Ted hosted a CCE-pilot meeting at a big Boston law firm to launch our work. Before they "discovered" charters, most of the big foundation and moneyed and politically connected adults were excited about pilots. When Ted spoke, last, his simple, reassuring brilliance pulled it all together.

For the next nearly twenty years, Ted served on the CCE board and helped CCE become an organization known for trusting educators to "provide the conditions and get out of the way," as Larry Myatt, then principal of the first Boston Coalition School-Fenway, remembers Ted as saying. As Larry went on to write me recently, "the poobahs were barely aware that he was endorsing difference as an asset, as a natural fact of schooling, and suggesting that the locus of decision making be the school." Ted was, in Larry's words, an organizer. Not a word Ted said was not true to his convictions and the work we committed ourselves to.

Ted's thinking was again brought to life in the mid-1990s as he and Nancy Sizer imagined and then helped construct their own "dream" school, along with friends and colleagues in their rural community—the Francis W. Parker Charter Essential School in Devens, Massachusetts—at just the time when I was moving to Boston to start a new K–8 school. There couldn't have been a better omen. When Ted and Nancy acted as co-principals in Parker's fourth year, we met often for dinner to discuss our challenges and delights, and even wrote a book, *Keeping School: Letters to Families from Principals of Two Small Schools* (Boston: Beacon Press, 2004) to explain our daily work.

• • •

As a reformer over many years, Ted was characterized by his enthusiasm—and his persistence. His style was refreshing. He never had answers. He simply talked aloud about what he knew—that the task of translating ideas and theories into life-size schools was a never-ending task. He knew that our work was important, that we were each trying our best under circumstances that we knew more about than he did.

(Actually, I began to doubt this.) Furthermore, we soon realized that he took it for granted that there was no finished
product. We'd be analyzing and creating—making revisions
upon revisions—for a lifetime and more. All our work together,
then and now, fit well into my understanding of democracy—
that respectful but messy idea that never finally gets it right.

PREFACE: THE LAY OF THE LAND

When I fly across our America—at least when the day is clear—I can look down and easily pick out the public high schools, the large, familiar, bulky buildings surrounded by playing fields and black-topped parking lots, some of these locations containing neat rows of yellow school buses. You cannot miss them. They are so ubiquitous that they are an integral and expected part of the country's landscape, familiar images that we all recognize coast to coast: *the lay of our land.*

These high schools, structurally similar but locally unique to their people in community after community all across America, should remind us that secondary schools such as these are one of this nation's most important social mechanisms, which, at their best, are models of democracy as well as providers of the intellectual and moral equipment for young people to survive and prosper in our culture. They are the oxygen of democracy: the one place where all of our adolescents, save some unlucky or neglected ones, have a chance to rub shoulders with young people both alike and different from themselves, a "melting pot," as the admirers of this country have termed our communities.

The sad fact remains, however, that the design of our beloved high school as we know it has run its course, no longer serving youth as well as it once did. Indeed, in many quarters, adolescents and the schools are today even a source of disdain, a piece of the entertainment industry that makes big money by trivializing growing up, mocking the inevitable awkwardness of this universal process, within and beyond school buildings.

We cannot escape that reality. That Americans transformed their nineteenth-century high schools and academies from a tiny group of wealthier or religiously driven institutions to places that enrolled the full teenage population was an extraordinary achievement. Free-thinking, engaged citizens—*educated people*—have long been the backbone of our culture, whether these young people lived in large cities or small towns, even hamlets in thinly populated townships. We should take satisfaction in that achievement. With hard and steady work, grassroots democracy can work.

However, if our current high schools are indeed ill-designed and inefficient, the question facing the current generation is *What next?* What can be done? Do we have the will to take on the big job that is needed to newly provide for the benefit of our young citizens, at full public expense, in ways that address the needs of the twenty-first century? We teachers need to protect what is endangered about our work, but also must add new tasks for ourselves because they are needed in our times, particularly by the vast numbers of disadvantaged children and the new ways of critical thinking that they will require to get on in the world. How can the American people prepare youth to cope with the sirens of a capitalist economy? If a place called "high school" is part of that response, what should be its mission and shape? After all these years, how can we pull off a change that challenges the past and asks us to think in new ways about growing up American?

The twentieth-century story of the spread of formal schooling for all American citizens is an extraordinary one. A comparable tale that we hope would be written fifty years from now is one that we should begin to sketch out, to use as a rough target. This book outlines one person's vision of what such a future secondary education might be. Whatever happens, whether it follows my plan or another, the task will require firmness, persistence, and wise flexibility.

· · ·

My plane hits the runway with a bump. Many of the passengers let out a breath of relief. The veteran riders wake up from their sleep and start collecting their belongings from the seat pockets and awkwardly stuff them into their briefcases, elbows knocking one another. They crowd into the airplane's narrow aisles, as though pushing ahead of other passengers would get them off faster. Ultimately we all shuffle our way out.

Even now, finally within the airport, with its impatient people coming and going to this place or that, I cannot get my earlier reverie out of my mind, and I ponder what we call a "high school" might be. I grieve a bit as I understand enough about schools today to know that their current design does not work well to meet this country's expectations, and, further, I know that many politicians and most educators appear not at all ready to undertake a fresh plan. We are stuck on the old metaphors and procedures, such as the use of time as coinage, indicating that the more important a subject is, the more time it will get. We inherited a program of studies that in its overall structure has not changed in over a century; we also inherited college- and university-based training for educators that is all too comfortable with the status quo even as its professors rail against it. There is irony here. Tinkering with what we have—a little reorganization here and a little addition there—will no longer work.

A friend suggests that the airlines themselves might be kin to the schools, places that served an earlier time but that are now outmoded. Much that we believed worked for us in our classrooms now seems less successful. Air travel worked for us, but much of the business for which we earlier flew can now be transacted over the Internet, for a tiny fraction of the earlier price.

Today I have no easy answers, no policies to suggest that are Guaranteed to Work, but I trust that the selections that follow—issues to tackle more than things to do—might suggest some sensible, persuasive moves to make. Much of what I have written here is, perhaps inevitably, a means of recollection, what a person who has labored in a field admires or finds embarrassing enough to share. At the same time, I believe that there is not, nor ever should be, one perfect educational system sent down from on high for America to put into place. Democracies should never be the seedbeds of autocratic, top-down control. Freedom is necessarily messy.

Perhaps we teachers and principals worry that we will get the new practice wrong and thus open ourselves up for more unsettling criticism. We have learned to keep our heads down and conspire primarily with our immediate colleagues. Sadly, we live today with flak coming at us from newspapers and school board meetings; some is valid, some not. Thus we are stuck, aware of our shortcomings and those of the modern technologies that teach powerfully but that at their worst distract from what the high school values, and are confused by how to react to them. However, if we get our act together, we can do better.

This book is one attempt to give shape to the needed agenda. It is an argument as much as an analysis. Like virtually all writing, even so-called nonfiction, the words that follow are affected by my own intellectual priorities and by what I have done in my life and during my career. I make no claim for total dispassion; this writing is in part a memoir, a personal odyssey. I care deeply about what follows here.

INTRODUCTION BY
NANCY FAUST SIZER

Ted Sizer was a communicator. His relationship with his readers was faithful and impassioned—on both sides. At the reception after his memorial service, I was doing pretty well at remembering people and their names, but I caught sight of a stranger in the long line and worried about him until he reached me. Was he from Harvard? Brown? Parker? The Coalition? Luckily, he didn't ask me if I remembered him, but he gave me a hug. "I read his books," he explained, never told me his name or anything else, and moved on.

Ted returned the favor. In the Horace books, he spoke from his own heart, determined to take on a complicated topic and describe it in such a way as to gather comrades for the work ahead. He founded the Coalition of Essential Schools to be the institution that would help to meet his—and his readers'—challenge. His operation for colon cancer in 2001 barely slowed him down, and *The Red Pencil* was published in 2004. In the months and years after his devastating diagnosis of metastatic cancer in 2005, he kept on working to keep himself and others abreast of what he was thinking. "I'm never sure of what I believe," he said, "until I have written it." Though he was terribly frustrated with computers—his long, broad fingers played havoc with keyboards, until we finally found the biggest one sold and put down cardboard barriers where his fingers weren't supposed to stray—they were actually designed for writers like him; they allowed him to write and rewrite to his heart's content. And he was very content with any day when there was time and energy enough to spend on his book.

After a few trial runs—many months spent considering and reconsidering vocabulary, for example, which has greatly influenced the book—he decided that he would like to advise others who were designing what they hoped would be successful schools, at least for the collections of students whom they would teach. We have known many such people at Brown and the Harvard Graduate School of Education and the Parker School, and this would help them change their schools or found new ones.

His book—and his advice—would encourage all of us who are interested in education that we are doing what he liked to call "the work of the Lord." Surely if there is any point to life, it is to nourish and prepare the next generation, as personally as possible. The book would consider policy only in the ways that it influences daily work, and in it are many ideas about how daily work might proceed. He was still very interested in policy, but toward the end of his career, he came back to its beginning, and to individual kids.

Along the way, partly because I nagged him about it, he added autobiographical details that explained the sources of many of his ideas. He was a very modest man, but I persuaded him that readers who knew more about his life would understand his message more deeply.

So here are his last thoughts. A few are about his illness, but that's where he was, in part, and his courage in facing it is part of his legacy. The rest of his thoughts were with you, those to whom he was speaking throughout, and with your futures—which, he felt sure, would be exciting and worthy ones. I hope you will feel that: what our daughter at his memorial service called "his hand on your shoulder." And I hope so very much that in reading this book you will appreciate another chance to keep company with this remarkable man.

CHAPTER · ONE

The Problem

A mericans have burdened themselves, however unintentionally, with a high school design that is inefficient and runs counter to an abundance of solid research about how formal learning in fact takes place. What were dogged improvements made by educators more than one hundred years ago clearly do not serve us well today.

This happy burden represents a paradox. We admire our national commitment to mass, inclusive secondary education, but at the same time we know that the current vehicles to deliver such an education do not function effectively. We persist with a head-in-the-sand attitude odd for a nation that is driven by a competitive economy. We are *for* the public schools (and nonpublic schools as well), but we appear to be *against* much of what they are doing. That is, we love the people in the schools, and the idea of schooling, even as we know that the places we have do not work all that well. We have lost our belief in what we think we believe. Many of us are embarrassed about that, but we keep our embarrassment to ourselves.

It's survival of the fittest out there in the American capitalist tradition. However, public education is meant to serve all children, including those who find both learning and schooling difficult. Some political critics call this commitment socialism, top-down control by bureaucrats. Despite our schools' readily identifiable shortcomings, accompanied by noisy mocking and criticizing of the schools, we carry on.

We have long believed that every American teenager deserves an education that will equip him or her for a lifetime of constructive activity. We responded over a century ago by creating a locally controlled system of secondary schools. The word *system,* itself, is instructive; it was not imposed by federal or state authorities; instead, it largely evolved in its details if not its structure. In community after community, citizens at the grassroots—the parents of the school-age children—organized their schools along lines that they felt were universally endorsed and thus could be considered the "best."

The process was at first hit or miss; a high school was started here but not there; one high school offered a rich program of offerings, another only the bare bones. The schools took root most quickly in the Northeast and Midwest in the latter part of the nineteenth century, as these areas of the country, especially in urban areas, had excess tax-raised money that could be used to erect a building and gather a principal and staff. In the early twentieth century, southern states were still recovering from the dislocations and costs of the Civil War, and their populations included many African

American citizens for whom schooling had to be provided from scratch. The notion of a mass, universally inclusive national education system took decades to establish and is still in motion, as witnessed by a surge in Latino populations from Mexico and elsewhere, carrying with them a mix of languages, customs, and expectations. There is energy in this, but the constantly differing demands challenge us—and should.

Over a century ago, our elected officials, with the citizens' blessing, decided to design the high schools on the basis of students' ages. ("If you are sixteen, you are most likely to be in eleventh grade.") A late-nineteenth-century nation dominated by farmers arranged for school to take place only during the nine months when teenagers were not needed in the fields. These predecessors organized the work of students and teachers into subjects, each occupying a block or two of designated time, each to be covered as prescribed by a common plan. By the 1920s, high school had come to be a kind of secular religion, and criticizing its basic design was therefore, in some quarters, a form of blasphemy.

Today, however, many of us no longer look at the secondary schools through such a loving, trusting lens. For example, even as we recognize that chronological age tells us something—but hardly everything—about a particular adolescent, we still adhere to "age grading." We see that all knowledge (however thoughtfully defined) is not easily "packaged," structurally conformed for familiar teaching and learning; it is more evolutionary than that. The high schools' academic curriculum of what we have come to call *courses* is familiar, each course covering a "subject" that, in its design and justification, would have been familiar to our great-grandparents—the staples of English, mathematics, science, history and social science, music and art. What thoughtful contemporary educators know, however, is that scholarly and educational tastes and habits are in constant motion, as experience, research, and changed social and political circumstances suggest new structures and procedures. Times change, even for guardians of tradition. Even some schools change, but many don't.

We are also stuck with yesterday's ideas of what a school's physical structure should be: a collection of rooms of equal size and shape under one roof, in which teaching and learning are expected to proceed, an egg crate of predictable places. Teachers in well-run modern schools can move, say, from room 2B to room 14C with the expectation that they would find all the conventionally accepted equipment that teachers need, such as sturdy wall-mounted blackboards, maps, charts, science equipment, and a well-stocked and relevant classroom library.

Here and there one finds new school structures, ones that could make different sorts of teaching and learning more likely than what is provided by the traditional designs. Some of these exceptions are seen in old buildings whose original function has disappeared and that are now newly fitted for modern education. Even this modification can be awkward for many classes, where a bend in the room makes it impossible for some students to see the blackboard. Still, if a school today has all sorts of electronic devices for teachers' and students' use—laptop computers, for example—the course can be covered in individualized or common ways, whatever the teacher needs—assuming that the school's fuses do not blow from overload.

However, if one visits high schools or the conferences organized by their leaders, one finds that behind all the bricks and mortar, the old, familiar assumptions of how school should be designed stubbornly remain: age grading, separated subjects, the agrarian calendar, and hierarchical management. Furthermore, permeating the atmosphere is the feeling that children learn by accreting information and content—the fill-up-the-brain metaphor—with the student being the empty vessel and the curriculum the liquid to be poured in. This content usually reflects the traditional disciplines of the late-nineteenth-century course of study, one that may have well served the expectations of parents and educators in the 1890s, but, when viewed with a fresh eye, appear oddly old-fashioned, in the pejorative sense.

The coinage of most schools is found in the minutes assigned to each class session, with the school's bell system telling teachers and students alike what to do and where to go, the assumption being that a single, time-driven system is necessary. In most schools today, we need only to listen to the bells; we do not need watches. If some students are late to class or running truant in the hallways, an assistant principal will likely nab them and, taking each by a metaphorical earlobe, drag the miscreants back to where they were supposed to be and make a note of all this for the record. In vast buildings crying out for crowd control, time and place often seem to be valued more than learning. Still, it's hard to focus on the material—and that's *learning*, isn't it?—if you're not in class but are roaming the hallways with friends.

As far as time goes, in most schools there is lenience for me, the teacher. If on some morning I am a bit late in getting to my classroom, I am rarely chided for my tardiness. However, if I am habitually late to class, I will be called to account. Our union representative will have an awkward case to build for my defense; habitual lateness on the part of teachers is unpopular in all quarters. Even if I do get to class on time, I cannot teach my students well if there is noisy chaos next door, arising from an unsupervised group of teenagers. Perhaps a certain deference to time and space is one old-fashioned assumption that has not lost its usefulness.

• • •

What is high school for in this day and age? For many children a century ago, high school, especially in rural areas, was one of the few places where they were confronted with unusual information and with abstractions—in the case of history and geography, with places and events that were wondrous to consider. Today's young people have the media close at hand—radio, television, a riot of options available on the Internet, some accurate and useful that any person can usefully pull up, others inaccurate and unwholesome. Our generation of adolescents, and surely those that will follow them far into the future, will inevitably be shaped by the largely for-profit media; the shows they watch on television and on the Internet will inevitably move them, excite them, amuse them—teach them. Some of these images will stick in their minds for years and will be more influential even than the neighborhoods in which they live. One purpose of a modern high school becomes to impart the ability to select wisely from among a cornucopia of alternatives.

Another purpose is to fill the teenagers' time. Many contemporary teenagers are prevented by law from working all but part-time jobs. Their parents, however, are mostly at work trying to provide for them. School is where kids can find each other and engage in extracurricular activities that may give them a sense of their own place in a serious, consequential community. They teach each other—for good or ill.

High school has traditionally been considered a relatively safe melting pot, the assumption embedded in school design being that each of us develops his or her personality and convictions in a predictable manner—rich kids, middle-class kids, poor kids all the same. The conventional wisdom is that good parents raise good kids. With whom our children play is a measure of how good we are. It affects the character of the schools to which we want them to go. Expectations in all sorts of places, from the richest to the poorest, are high: "These are my kids. Of course they will be good. I am good . . ." Parents will usually be advised to calm down: "Don't worry; they will grow out of this silliness." School can help them understand, accept, and properly raise their kids.

School may help with the *fear* that is so often present in most adolescents' lives and has been there for many decades. When our sons and daughters move from middle school to high school, a somewhat different set of standards are applied to each of them—and thereby to their parents. "What'll I be when I grow up?" a youngster may ask herself. She may hear the familiar jibe, "Don't be so *junior high*." She knows that her older family members are wondering about all this too: "What will Emily become? Will she be successful?" with success defined as financial and physical security, a warm family life full of her children, and a well-developed and respectable ego.

Adolescents fear conflict, not particularly that in competitive athletics, but beyond school. "Will I make enough money to be able to do what I want with my life?" "Will I get a job when I graduate? Or should I go to Iraq or Afghanistan or wherever is the next battleground to kill others and be killed by them?" Many adults have little awareness of these worries, or repress them when they emerge. What they see and hear are smiling kids and noisy chatter, activity that masks the young person's feelings, sometimes even from themselves.

There is no quick fix for these matters, no dependable scheme that will accomplish what the society writ large expects of parents and adolescents. One can jiggle a school's plans, one can test that scheme, one can inveigh against it, but the fact remains that there is no easily described plan ready to be put into place that can meet all the conventional expectations.

What will it take to compete with the popular media, particularly television and the Internet, that bottomless pit of information, misinformation, and distortion? These powerful and largely for-profit ("Somebody else's profit, not mine!" the aware student will say) influences are not going away. The companies that sell messages are too powerful, too useful, and too profitable for contemporary cultures to ignore. We cannot return to the nineteenth century when silences, except the songs of birds and the thunder of an approaching storm, were the expected, unchallenged reality.

Politically, we teachers must try to persuade citizens that we all *do* have a problem, and that the puzzle is complex. No one likes to be told that he is not all that he could be. Save for the morosely uncertain, most citizens say—or pretend—that they know what they need to know. If you, dear reader, do not believe this, go to the city council or town meeting in your community. All sorts of people there become experts on anything from the bus schedule to the efficiency of boilers for the gymnasium to the correct intake of calories at the school kitchen. It is democracy in action, with all its messiness, posturing, and endless absorption of time. It is not rule by self-appointed and formally credentialed experts.

• • •

Do we need better teachers? What is meant by better? More demanding? Can we hire appealing persons who can draw a teenager into their own work? If a school had a retired star from the New England Patriots on its coaching staff, he could be a magnet. "Want to know what it is to train?" he might ask. "You have to know yourself, how tall or short you are, how ready you are to handle pain, how willing you are to make weekend and summer training camps. Still, after all this, you may fail to make the team, since a new student just arriving is a quicker, bigger halfback than you will ever be. However, a team's reserves have responsibilities too." Do we want our coaches and teachers to be inspirational? Is this wish unrealistic? Realistic? Both?

We have to think not just about teachers but the content and skills that they are to provide. Do schools need new curricula? Should we keep the framework of the existing courses, giving each a careful face-lift? Or should we develop some new programs, created by a committee that carefully gauges the strengths and weaknesses of each member of the faculty and the needs, aspirations, and willingness to work hard of each of its students? Or should we offer a simple set of courses—domains, some would call them, or fields of study? If the higher-ups, such as the state leaders who are being prodded by the federal government and its No Child Left Behind Act, tell us what we must teach and threaten us with tests, is there still some wiggle room? Maybe we should have two courses of study: one test prep wholly focused on what we believe to be the upcoming, governmentally imposed examinations and the other one that makes sense to us, to our particular students, and accommodates the wishes of our community.

Do we need to divide the allotted classroom time differently than we do at present? If we stay with the idea of an extended summer vacation, can we usefully attach ourselves to kindred organizations and enterprises, such as working farms? Many such places need extra hands at harvesting time, even recruiting them from Mexico and paying them well on a piecework basis. ("The more bushels of firm, ripe apples you pick, the more you earn.") Would such an example increase the motivation of a broad variety of students?

Can we insist that only the students we want are to be admitted to our school, on our teachers' terms? There may be practical reasons for this—for example, a small, poorly financed school may be able to offer only a few courses at the depth the school expects. Admission may therefore turn on what a particular student wants and needs and on the interest of the faculty to address those needs and interests. Many small, private, and parochial (religious) schools make this decision by necessity. Some schools by design admit students only on the basis of their apparent academic strength, this measured by formal examinations. The Boston Latin School, a public school founded in 1635, is an example of this. Yet others admit students on the basis of space available at grade level and stated interest on the part of the family to attend. Many public schools may say that they admit anyone without exception, but the obvious restraints—space in the school building, geography, existence of public transport, family preferences—apply nonetheless.

Can we open our doors to all and, ideally, varied students? Can we teachers offer courses that we want to offer and teach these courses in new ways that appeal to us? No, as the foregoing argument attests. Or at least, not completely. The world is never that simple. However, mindlessly accepting the existing historical constraints is no better an answer.

• • •

Can we create a new American culture? The task seems formidable, considering the power of those who rule our current social order, which is dominated by the hard realities of capitalism. Capitalism has many flaws as a means to economic and social order and justice, but I believe that its political design—ideally, a responsiveness to consumers—can provide the flexibility that successful schools (and families) need. Capitalism indeed has many faults; it is just that other systems have more faults.

Paradoxically, perhaps, what is preferable and even practical in theory may be very difficult to achieve in practice. Board members will suddenly become cautious. "Yes, we agreed that our district needs a face-lift, but how fast can we move—and still get reelected?" Some parents will get nervous, or at the least interested, even intrigued. Many of them will believe that they know what school is; they went to one, and many remember it fondly, warts and all.

Educational authorities, many of whom will talk a reform game, might get skittish when it is clear that there are some—even many—parents and teachers who are persuaded by these particular newfangled ideas, and they may yet slide off of the issue by suggesting that the proponents of something different start a new school or schools—charter, pilot, or other alternative approach—thereby keeping the critics so busy planning and arguing about a new venture that they may fade out of the public eye. This is likely a poor strategy for those who want to stem the tide of new schools; the press will pick up the story of the happy possibilities of some of these freshly designed places, thereby spreading the possibility of options. *Options!* And choice among them! In this lies a real revolution: what once may have seemed impossible in a land of monopolies is no longer as unthinkable today.

• • •

This problem of discomfort with the status quo is not new. Americans have faced these problems head-on in an earlier time. Conditions some decades ago were quite similar. Families using the conventional schools gradually became disenchanted with them. Professionals working within them were increasingly restless, even embarrassed by their familiar work at existing schools; they harbored a sense that something better was possible. In 1983, a nongovernmental commission gathered, including A. Bartlett Giamatti, the president of Yale University; Glenn T. Seaborg, Nobel laureate; and William O. Baker, chairman of the board of the Bell Laboratories. The commission's report was titled *A Nation at Risk: The Imperative for Educational Reform*; its recommendations were wise, a step forward. Although leaders during the 1980s failed to act, the current generation would benefit from pondering what those commissioners said, why they said it, and why it fizzled almost months after its release.

Those earlier misgivings and anxieties suggested that political conditions were ripe for action. Fortunately, the same conditions may apply today. Many families are restless. They want real choices from among strong schools for their children. This makes the task of school designers much easier, even compelling. We educators have more friends than we may realize. They must be organized. We and they must create schools that are familiar enough so as not to scare people away but bold enough to reflect the hopes and expectations of the parents of school-age children.

• • •

Thus is the problem. The solution will be costly, especially in the time we have committed to the effort. We must go to work on practical remedies now with all speed. What should a truly *new* secondary school look like? What will make it new? What from the past should remain supported and in place? I try here to answer some of these questions in an order that might make my case clear and thus persuasive. My arguments depend heavily on carefully chosen words: language drives action. And not all good ideas are new ideas. We must protect the best of the past and discard that which no longer serves our particular children well. It will take plenty of nerve on all our parts to find new, better ground.

CHAPTER · TWO

Growing Up American

Change is not easy for anyone, especially for an adolescent. The process is messy, full of pressures, defeats, and successes.

Being a parent is hardly easier. "My nice little child is changing before my very eyes," one says. "He doesn't want to cuddle anymore; he seems almost offended by me. He is petulant and thinking beyond his competence. He argues, 'I *can* take care of myself.' My daughter appears to be in a permanent grump. She looks right through us when she returns from school, gets a bottle of 7-Up from the refrigerator, stomps off to her room, and then slams the door. I feel like a hotel employee in my own home, serving the young at their beck and call, and expecting few tips, or even a 'thank you'!"

Sometimes I-now-the-adult have had it up to my ears with the young. I ride the subway to and from work, and I dread the times that our car will be invaded by teenagers, going to or coming from their high schools. They seem to talk all at once, creating an annoying babble. They appear to understand what each is saying; I don't. They might be speaking a strange language that only they know, peppered with names I have never heard before. Many wear backpacks jammed with their clothes and books, and as they clutch the straps hanging from the car's ceiling, they heedlessly spin around, those backpacks whacking me in the face. A few say "sorry" but continue with their conversations, certain to be whacking sitting passengers again.

Periodically I wonder how I was raised. I survived adolescence, and my parents also appear to have survived. Eventually I learned to accept the reality that some issues in life are not explainable, that there are no clear answers, that the social context in which each person grows up is not only different from that of others but changing rapidly. We cannot stop time.

Growing up as a definable stage in life has long caught the attention of scholars. One of the earliest investigators was Granville Stanley Hall in the late nineteenth century at Clark University in Worcester, Massachusetts. Edgar Z. Friedenberg's 1959 study of teenagers, *The Vanishing Adolescent*, picked up the theme. Vanishing adolescence might be—for most if not all young Americans—the end of a time of life largely free of obligations save to obey their parents, show up at school with their homework completed, earn their own pocket money to spend on a candy bar or a comic book, and steer clear of activity that might interest the police.

The stereotypical middle-class family—the staple of tepid afternoon television tales inhabited by Mom, Dad, Sis and Bro, and Cuddles, the dog that was completely housebroken— is not and never was. Such a "growing up" has never really existed, especially for young people from low-income families, overstressed or one-parent families, or families (of whatever income group) where coarse cursing, say, is the principal language medium or where family members are crippled by alcoholism and drug use. Being a child can be difficult, and it is a wonder that most of the youngsters survive. Some do not, alas, and are often treated as outcasts (even as they may actually like this semi-invisibility) in a society that has the traditions and wealth to help every emerging American have a fair shake in life, but that does not live up to its promise.

• • •

One might prefer to think that parents and children must be loving, empathic, and helpful allies in the family's march across time. Yet to accept this mirage is a sure way to become disillusioned. Actually, growing up is more complicated—and, in fact, far more interesting—than all that.

I myself had a happy childhood. My family consisted of my parents, five daughters, and then me, *finally* the male. My father is reputed to have said, "A boy in time saves nine." (I don't know if my mother heard him, or what she would have thought if she had!) We lived on a working farm in Bethany, Connecticut, near New Haven, with a large measure of outdoor help from a Ukrainian anti-Communist refugee family who occupied a small farmhouse on the far side of our property. Every other day, Frank Nachuk delivered us milk, cream, and eggs from his animals. Frank also provided the flat, thick stone boat drawn by his two enormous workhorses. My father, a professor of the history of art and director of the Yale Art

Gallery, loved to build stone walls—"stone art," it might legitimately be called—one of the most complicated examples of which was the retaining wall that kept our front lawn from washing down the hill before it. Building that retainer—which today still exists precisely as it did in 1940, with every rock solidly in place—was an extraordinary bit of artistic exercise, tough on the back and the fingers and demanding the almost three-dimensional imagination necessary to lodge a secure rock on all six sides, the result producing a tight fit. Frank found rocks that filled my father's description and hauled them over to him. "Practical art," my father called it.

My mother ruled the roost: "Mum's the boss; do as she demands . . . now" was my father's retort whenever I complained that my mother had set me an unpleasant chore, such as killing the turkeys before Thanksgiving. The turkeys were indeed scary. They were difficult to catch and fought back bravely. They looked me in the eye (or so I believed) as I wrestled each of them to the ground. "*She* told me to *do it*," I explained to them, as I hacked away with a sharp axe. Those murders still give me vague nightmares. I imagine the fowls staring at me as I prepare my swing at their necks. Growing up can leave such scars.

To help with our large family, we were joined by a German woman, Anne-Liese Wellershaus, whom my parents had met in Europe in 1929 (before my sister Alice and I were born) when the entire family visited art galleries, primarily in Germany and Austria. After helping the family twice in Germany, Anne-Liese agreed to come to the United States just before I was born in 1932. She was a quiet but fierce anti-Nazi; she wanted no part of Adolph Hitler's Reich; my parents admired her pluck and her convictions and were grateful for the devotion that she showed to each of us, especially to Alice and me. In Bethany, besides watching us when Mum was busy with the older girls, she did some indoor cleaning, washing, and cooking chores; she also raised chickens and sold their eggs to neighbors. After I went to school, she went back to Germany, but found that her country and her family were torn apart by Nazism. She returned to us but got a job—via my mother's quietly used contacts, which were necessary, as Anne-Liese had never graduated from any sort of secondary school—as an aide to a kindergarten teacher at the Foote School in New Haven. By all reports, she was very good at this. The little kids loved her and tumbled all over her. She was endlessly patient with them.

Alice and I were sent to elementary school early, in my case at just five. This might have been to allow Anne-Liese to return to Germany. Another reason might have been that the youngest children in large families are often considered more advanced than they in fact are. We knew a lot; the family's dinner conversation was very adult and serious even as most of it was over our heads. Anne-Liese continued to live with us and provided a link between the elders and the children.

The Foote School, where Anne-Liese taught, was named for its first principal, a Mrs. Foote. It was a place that then could be called "soft traditional," an institution that was warm and welcoming but also rigidly programmed (kindergarten through eighth grade), offering the traditional subjects of English, mathematics, history, some art (painting and drawing), and a tad of science, all largely taught out of textbooks for nine years in a low-key, unthreatening way. The classes were more progressive than the syllabus suggested; we made maps and charts as relevant topics came up. A standard eighth-grade exercise for each of us was the creation of a large, carefully labeled map of the Chaucerian path taken by religious folk as they wended their way through Hampshire, via Winchester, to the shrine of Thomas à Becket in Kent. Most of us found this mapmaking exercise very engaging, especially for the one or two boys who struggled with language and would today be diagnosed with special needs.

The Foote School—in those days a refitted old two-story garage, hardly a magnificent structure—for me was full of happy hours. I made some good and lasting friends, especially one, Robert Jessen by name, who was a talented woodworker, but a struggler with the standard basics. The teachers had carefully found an area where Bobby could excel—art—providing me now with an early example of how a subject that was not considered traditionally academic could grab an imagination and thereby instill some important basic habits and skills. Bobby and I spent hours making models of naval fleets and tank battalions, and playing war on the smooth linoleum floors of a bedroom in Bethany. We tried to re-create what we believed to be real battles, with armadas led by Admirals Halsey and Spruance. In effect, we were in our own (all-too-naive) worlds, full of wonder and wonderings, however in fact violent. Our parents tolerated this dreaminess and made no complaint that we were wasting our time. No standardized test faced us on a rigid time schedule based wholly on our ages.

Like many others of my age, mine was a childhood highly affected by World War II. My father had the (now)

old-fashioned idea that men, except those who were physi-
cally crippled, should enlist in the military. He enlisted shortly
after Pearl Harbor around the time of his fiftieth birthday.
With some other art professors, he ended up in the Monuments, Fine Arts, and Archives section, whose aim was to
prevent the destruction of art through intricate ground-level
diplomacy. He worked in North Africa and Italy and then was
sent to England to ready himself for the invasion of France.
There he grew ill and was sent home before the war ended.
My growing number of brothers-in-law also saw active service
either in Washington or overseas.

Back in Bethany, my mother and Anne-Liese held down
the fort; it was definitely their war too. They had loving friends
and family on both sides of the conflict, and felt enormous
empathy for each other. They raised Alice and me, kept in
touch with the other daughters, saved on rationing by having
Anne-Liese drive us to school, kept animals and an enormous
garden (much of the products of which they canned), and did
all the work the Nachuks and others used to do. Anne-Liese,
who had become a U.S. citizen in 1940, was part of a telephone
network of air wardens; Mum worked for the Red Cross, and
told more than one parent about the death of his or her son.
When my father was sent home, they slowly and lovingly
nursed him back to health. All this was done with courage,
stability, and even moments of enjoyment and humor; I marvel
now at how normal they kept our lives.

There seemed to be a purpose to this war, and they didn't
consider themselves victims, at least around me. The lingo of
the day included, front and center, the word *service*, as in "In
what service are you enrolled?" That word's connotations are

different in our day: one elects to join one of the armed services, signing up for the perks or out of confusion over what to do next. Too many of us appear to be comfortable with the statement that "everyone should serve—except my son or daughter."

In 1945, at the end of the Foote School's eighth grade, I was shipped off to my father's alma mater, Pomfret School, in then-rural northeastern Connecticut. Its student body largely comprised white, Protestant Christians (or those who pretended they were Protestants). Weekday evening and Sunday chapel services were required, with attendance taken.

This was where my relative youth and immaturity caught up with me. I was homesick, and struggled there academically and socially, in what in the long run was a useful experience, as it made me sympathetic to the terror that all sorts of students in all forms of secondary schools inevitably experience, now as well as then. Over and over I tried out for varsity and junior varsity sports teams, but never persuaded any coach to use me—a substantial expression of physical incompetence in a tiny school that needed every ambulatory body on its playing fields. I did, however, become the editor of the school newspaper, *The Pontefract,* and promptly got into trouble by editorializing that there should be some black students among us (though I used the then-acceptable term "Negroes"). The headmaster, Dexter Strong, was careful with me; he did not ban that issue; I believe now that he had long pressed the trustees to allow him to admit students other than white Christians but that his approaches had been met with repeated refusals. My editorial signaled that it was not only he who wanted a more diverse student population. In a curious way, Strong and I were allies, and we kept in contact in later years.

Entrance to Yale College followed (on full scholarship, as I was a faculty son, a perk that Yale staff were provided), where I completed an undistinguished major in English. I was dutiful but utterly uninspired (and probably, for my professors, uninspiring). Yale's English curricula at that time reflected the more-is-better mind-set; for example, in but a single term's time, we were set to read every word written by or ascribed to Geoffrey Chaucer in the original Middle English, with a one-page paper due at each class commenting on the assigned passage. I remember each of those classes as a weary trudge. Over the course of four years, we English majors climbed up the historical calendar, moving at an academic trot to Milton, Auden and more, and finally to T. S. Eliot. I remember little of all that to which I was exposed, save its unspoken but clear pedagogical message: it is more important to cover material than it is to become engaged with it.

When I stand back and reconsider this traditional and predictable *cursus honorum,* I am struck again by how well intentioned yet misguided it was, and in many high schools and colleges still is, much though their deans and presidents may deny it. In a conventional way, it did build character—"keep a stiff upper lip and do as you are told"—if only because it taught us that each one of us, without exception, had to slog through tedious topics as well as those matters that caught our imaginations.

My education depended on promotion merely on the basis of age and seat time. When I turned fifteen, I was assumed to know more than I did when I was fourteen. Of course, no two of us learn the canon (the word that the professoriat used and still uses to define the substantive core of their discipline, a path along which undergraduates must trudge, at least after freshman year) in the same way and at the same pace.

How I was taught depended almost entirely on the concept of *delivery*; I was told what I was to know by means of a teacher's voice, assisted, perhaps, by a blackboard or some sort of electronic device. Knowledge rolled in—it was and, too often still is, assumed—quite like a delivery truck dispensing goods that I have ordered from a catalogue.

Most of what is to be dispensed came at me in the form of *subjects,* those entities arising from past scholarship reflecting widely accepted areas of study as blessed by the academic gurus of the late nineteenth century, such as Harvard's then president Charles William Eliot. Again, its substance came largely from British writers; American authors were deemed to be rough colonials whose writing was, therefore, unworthy; writers from countries and traditions other than British were wholly absent. In all, I was a creature of that time; I respect what I was offered then, but I believe that I have learned to know better now, as I write this in 2009. My growing up was not typical, of course, World War II or not: I had a secure home life, doting family members, and decent schools to attend.

Although today I would like to bring lessons from my own learning into my teaching, I find many of the same restraints that my teachers had—and a few new ones. I-the-teacher-today know that the coinage of schooling was and is, for almost all students, the passage of time ("hours devoted by all and sundry"), and, accordingly, I must think about my work with the clock in mind. The more minutes my students engage with teachers like me, the more they are expected to know and thus to be able to demonstrate for us, not only on exams set by and in the schools but also through the assessments set by local, state, and federal governments. I am to be measured largely on the basis of my students' success on standardized, machine-graded, pencil-and-paper tests.

As a result, in most schools, the curriculum comprises what teachers believe will be on those tests. The teacher's task is not to think through what knowledge might be most compelling or useful for her particular students but to make good guesses on what the upcoming set of tests might include and to teach toward that material. If we refuse to do that test-prep work, we can be subjected to the complaints of parents (and of some students) that we have let them down. Thus is the curriculum of my neighborhood school imposed largely, if sometimes subtly, by authorities far from my school and fully beyond my influence, largely cast as mini-bites of content, which they say is what this country needs.

Like my own teachers when I was young, most commonly I do my teaching alone. No one sees or hears me save my students. My adult colleagues and I share a cup of coffee in what is usually called the Teachers' Room, and we trade stories about our students as well as about our lives outside school. However, when the bell rings, it's back to just me and my thirty or so teenagers. The Teachers' Room is abruptly silent, almost empty.

The typical school day is still about six hours long. However, much of what we teachers try to do is jostled in our pupils' heads by the media with which most teenagers connect in the hours beyond school, everything from the soaps to car racing programs (with their fiery smashups) to educational television such as that presented by the government-protected nonprofit media, principally the Public Broadcasting System and National Public Radio. However, even these latter, well-intentioned enterprises depend for much of their funding on the generosity of business sponsors who influence what we and our students see and hear. Our programs are subtly an extension of a commercial agenda. I accept this because the alternative to a government-directed use of public programming would likely be infinitely worse. I just wish that business (to the extent that it can be presented as a monolith) had a more sophisticated understanding of what our schools are and might be.

Today's America has more than its share of stressed families. Also important, my generation in its youthful years did not have—or even foresee—the miracle first of television (*Sesame Street* had not been invented yet) and, more recently, of the Internet, that bottomless pit of good sense and nonsense. Where we live is not much of a constraint now. I now may learn, good stuff and bad, from all quarters of this globe, all at my and my children's disposal at the click of a mouse, a new form of formal school.

All this new technology affects how and what our young people learn. School today is far more than merely a bricks-and-mortar place with classrooms staffed by teachers who stand before their students with a blackboard at their backs. The delivery system (the widely used metaphor is itself instructive) was tell-and-then-show-me, over and over again. If a student is dutiful, she takes down notes about what is being presented and stores them in three-ring binders. She does not want to make waves, and she longs be an honors student and thus able to attend a prestigious college.

In its stubborn practice, at least, this delivery system is clearly obsolete today. Thanks to communication technology, each of us, even the youngest, has access to all sorts of information. Educators' tasks must be to separate the wheat from the chaff in that enormous jumble of ideas, facts, and opinions, to extract the true from the untrue and the useful from the merely entertaining. To be effective, then, a school should take a wholly new form, one that we are only just realizing that we must invent. However, most public policy today continues to rest on the old delivery model, and the standardized testing that is the principal driver of subject matter in today's schools is little more than the old textbook in new and higher-stakes form. Fact-stuffing students' lives, albeit tested in new ways.

• • •

As I moved along in my career, I learned to use a variety of delivery systems, however old-fashioned they were. At Phillips Academy, Andover, where I served as headmaster for nine years, I found that the Socratic method—teaching by the use of a string of carefully chosen questions—worked well. I taught mostly eleventh and twelfth graders who could handle it. I did not relay information but, rather, pummeled them with questions that ultimately sent them off to the library— which, happily, had the depth of a liberal arts college—in search of the answers. Because Andover was a boarding school for all but a few day students who lived near the campus, some of whom were faculty children, I was able to keep close tabs on the students' work, assist the strugglers, and provoke the high fliers.

At Brown, the next step in my teaching career, I taught a lecture-and-section course on recent American educational history. I used the device of giving students early in the course an open question, such as "How does existing educational practice serve the ends of a free, democratic society?" In the large lecture meetings (two hundred–plus enrollees), I investigated relevant topics and events in American schooling over the last one hundred years. I had a nice passel of assistants, most of whom were graduate students in history, American civilization, and English as part of the Master of Arts in Teaching program, who met their sections weekly and reviewed the undergraduates' papers. In section meetings, my TAs would ask their students to lay out specifically what they thought were likely essential questions. Having to frame those questions deepened their knowledge of and respect for this interrogatory device. When foundation funds were available, we traveled to New York City, Hartford, and places where the school administrators were willing to open their schools to my students' listening, seeing, and asking questions. I was lucky in the schools we chose: I was thereby able to visit several sparkling educators, such as Dennis Littky, then at the tiny Thayer High School in the financially strapped small rural community of Winchester, New Hampshire, and Deborah Meier at New York City's Central Park East Secondary School. We all have been close and cordial friends ever since.

The move back to Harvard's Graduate School of Education in the late 1990s provided me (and Nancy; by this time we cotaught our course) with a new student population, graduate students, mostly in education but with a smattering of others over the years from the Kennedy School of Government, the divinity school, and, to our surprise, the architecture school. We asked each student to come up with what for him or her was what we called a "burning question" about learning and teaching (for example, "What differences in high school practice should obtain for students of differing social classes and language groups?"). Though we read several books in common during the yearlong seminar, all the writing was focused around finding ways to answer these individuals' questions. Each of these questions was, of course, unique, but the last assignment in the course involved small teams that tackled similar burning questions.

All of this was about my growing up as a teacher; these were new practices for me and a broadening of my sense of what education was. My work grew more and more progressive in that it focused on what the student saw as important rather on an already established canon.

To a foreigner, all this must appear astonishing. Our political leaders love to call the work of our educational system world class, this while school leaders in near and far-off places are in fact creating imaginative new systems that use contemporary technologies to teach worthy old skills. Progressive American industry builds up-to-date employee training into its everyday plans; at its best, each employee thus becomes an inventor, whose ideas help the company move forward. Ironically, we educators are expected, and often required, to be respectful of American business practices, constantly seeking how these may be used to improve our teaching and thereby the students' learning. We are asked, with some justification, to be more businesslike, but without the research and development moneys and employee training that are staples of American industry, and with little of the running room available in progressive businesses.

The formal educational system—including most of the schools of education from which one would reasonably expect work that countervailed against the inept status quo—often acts as if it is oblivious to all this. We professors largely train for the schools we have, whatever their flaws, rather than for the schools we should have. Perhaps our system is so familiar that thoughts of other approaches do not cross our minds; the traditional image of schooling is so dominant that no other vision or metaphor representing the learning of our young pops up. Americans have decided that we shall have schools and that we will keep our country's youngsters busy for five of each week's days, for at least nine months of each year.

We can do better.

So, *what, in fact, might be better?* First, all of us, parents and guardians especially, must pay attention. We must know what is going on in our schools and why, and we must spend time helping our children as they pass up the school ladder. All adults should try to get into the habit—when they become uncles and aunts, next-door neighbors, social service professionals, politicians—of looking out for young people. Earlier Americans did so seemingly instinctively. Those babies who survived the first, fragile months and years of life were put to work as soon as they had some abilities, the girls in kitchens, the boys in agriculture or even into the factories (where they were sometimes abused, overworked, and dismissed if they could not tolerate the working conditions). Despite these examples of harshness, work was part of growing up. Every family member had a role to play. Every child was expected to exhibit growth.

Public policies should continue to reflect this. Parents must keep abreast of what is happening in local boards, state legislatures, and Washington, to keep the pressure on for sound, flexible, and humane policies. The sustained publicity given to the so-called No Child Left Behind Act is a good example of the attention that is needed, as it forces individuals, organized groups of persons (lobbies), and professional associations such as the teachers' and administrators' unions to stay informed about legislation and the programs and practices emerging from that legislation, whether supporting their ideas or resisting them. NCLB's dependence on standardized tests is hard to excuse when looking at the research now available from such scholars as Howard Gardner and Mihaly Csikszentmihalyi.

State boards of education, where authority has been centered for over a hundred years, must today design an outline (that is, a sort of catalogue of what needs to be presented and assessed) of a desired, usually required, course of study that is described only generally, a minimal framework, thereby giving scope to family or local ideas and commitments to the specifics that seem best for their particular children. These "frameworks" should be provocative, specifically designed to provoke good ideas from the grass roots. State authorities should periodically inspect our work to ensure that we have not strayed too far from what is expected. There will be (and is) stress in this balanced system, but it is likely that any other form of assessment would be worse.

State moneys must be available to families of school-age children on the basis of family need (that is, taking into account family resources available to support their children and providing special support for children with learning disabilities). If critics want to call these resources the hated vouchers, so be it. Financial and political incentives are needed for clusters of families to create their own schools—call them charter or "in-district" alternative schools—thereby acting in harmony with a community's plans. (Indeed, if a community has no harmony, the school might provide it.) If possible, schools should work closely with their nearby public libraries. State authorities must regularly visit these schools and libraries to ensure that their intent and practice are up to snuff.

Many citizens will find these remedies to be threatening, even bizarre. As I write this, I can hear the shouts of derision. This will be *too new!* (Newness is always uncomfortable, as it threatens what "works.") Parents will say, *Don't do any experimenting with my kid!* These and comparable protests are reasonable and will surely be heard. However, there are counterarguments to be made, many of them on the basis of widely accepted policies in fields other than schooling.

First, there are long-standing precedents in local and state practice. Because driving cars is both an expression of personal freedom and a communal activity, sensible arrangements are required. There are lanes, crosswalks, traffic lights—all restricting personal freedom but enhancing the safety of more than just the driver. Drivers' licenses are mandatory for legal drivers; there are courses available to prepare for the standardized drivers' tests, and in order to obtain such a license, the applicant must pass a culminating driving test on real roads and in a variety of traffic conditions. These licenses, accepted by the American public, are analogous to those found in our national and state medical system, allowing emergency access to any and all public hospitals and medical practice. There is financial support for those who may need it, especially the elderly and the poor, through Medicare and Medicaid. All hospitals are inspected by state experts on a regular basis, protecting those who use them. These kinds of requirements and regulations tie together the needs of the public with the private persons and public and private institutions that seek to meet those needs. Our New American High School can learn from their successes and struggles.

Second, there is the example of free—that is, federally financed—education for military veterans. I, for example, paid little save special fees to the Harvard Graduate School of Education for my entire career as a student in my Master of Arts in Teaching and PhD in American history and education programs. The dollars provided were calculated on the basis of my twenty-one months of active-duty service in the Army. Americans accepted these funds as an appropriate payback for service to our country. Such help could also be offered to persons of modest means and education who seek a career in teaching.

Third, the existence of this largely local, messy, varied, largely independent movement lessens the likelihood of a stifling and politicized national system that rams a particular brand of ideas, these expressing a single ideology, down the throats of individual families and communities. There is strength for democracy in decentralization, however messy it is.

My point here needs stressing: these sorts of independent options may upset the leaders of an omniscient state or federal administration that decides that it, above all others, knows what is *best* for children. Although there is little evidence that any state government, much less the national government, has such a full-blown, draconian plan in mind, the opportunities for top-down direction are all too available. The closest we have come is represented by NCLB, legislation that is full of good intentions but, especially in its execution, has become stifling in how those intentions are translated into daily practice in schools.

The messiness and variety inherent in policies that give substantial power to the communities closest to specific children and their teachers are far preferable to any sort of tidy system. Bureaucracies value tidiness. Policymakers and their servants appear to want no surprises. However, necessary reform must be at the grass roots, just as it was over a century ago. It *will* be messy, but constructive messiness is the cost of freedom. Growing up is often a painful, if energizing, process, and growing up today may take subtly different but important forms than those with which we are accustomed. It also is fascinating, and many parents of teenagers enjoy the most difficult and simultaneously most interesting and rewarding times of their life.

The leaders of every New American High School must understand and honor this. Without knowing about families—each one with youngsters in a school or in a school within a large institution—teachers, counselors, and administrators will stumble often, hurting or improperly ignoring some young people. Our students are growing up. We must help them with this task, but not too much. Let them experiment. Let them find themselves, in current argot. However, we must attend to them, one by one, in the way that best serves each one.

Can this be done in large high schools? Yes, if they are broken down into human-scale units. Yes, if no teacher has too many students for him or her to know each one well. Can't we have rules, a teacher may ask, and insist that the kids obey them, thereby getting into the habit of doing the right thing? Yes, there must be rules in schools, but they must be sensitively worded and carefully followed and, when fresh evidence is available, changed. Common values about some matters will arise from necessary convenience. As they say, growing up ain't easy, but it cannot be avoided.

We old-timers know of this. Some of the kids come back to see us, at least those whom we apparently touched in a way that made a difference. Hearing their stories can be a source of exquisite joy. We just may have made a difference, and for the better.

CHAPTER • THREE

Learning

earning is what most of us believe schools should be about. Learning—at least good learning—should be cumulative, one skill or idea building on another. It must stick, meaning that is so deeply in the mind that it will be readily at hand when we need it.

Much of the formal detail that we learned in school—however good or not-so-good students we were—was simply stuff, trotted out, but not because of its clear intrinsic importance. Our teacher provided particulars with which we worked to sharpen our minds, and, our teacher hoped, this process provoked within us habits that would stick with us throughout our lives. "The foot pedal is next to the accelerator, itself a 'pedal' but a different shape." Of course, not every detail will stick for me, but the odds are that what had been earlier learned will reemerge: Turkey is in both Europe and Asia; how could I have forgotten!

Students of all ages (adults as well as children) vary in their condition of "stickiness." We all of any age get distracted and do not think to put our memories to work. Teachers can increase the stickiness by signaling a matter's importance. "We are going over important material here, so you must pay close attention. You may be tested on this"—a familiar and gentle threat. Even more effective are the connections that can be made between, for example, today's assignment on how a bill becomes a law and next week's trip to the state house, where appointments have been made so that students can explain why a specific law in which they are interested is desirable or undesirable. This information is undeniably sticky.

It is true that one function of schools is to babysit (to use an image that some will find demeaning), thus giving Mom or Dad some time off to go to work or even to do what they decide to do (such as writing books like this one) without keeping one ear ready to rush to a youngster's aid. Children take time—and rightly so. "Mom, this string is tangled up," and soon you are in the frustrating business of loosening and then unwinding a jumbled sphere of twine. "Dad," the impatient child blurts (with no appreciation that a parent almost surely has a task of his own under way that he feels is also important), "How do you get this little car cranked up so that it will go?" With most young children, the questions never cease, and happily so: Who wants a child who has little interest in the mysteries around him or her? "Why don't the fish drown?" is an example of an apt question, and one that many parents may find difficult to answer.

If a young child does *not* pepper you with questions, you should worry. He is not *learning*. Most parents, however, appreciate the fact that much of the child's learning occurs in school and that they must reinforce that work.

• • •

The dictionary definition of *learning* is clear and to the point: "An understanding and grasp of a habit of mind." A "learned" person is one who is "erudite; who possesses or demonstrates profound, often systematic knowledge."

The closest I ever came to being learned—a person who treasures scholarship almost for its own sake—was in graduate school. My experiences in the military solidified my wish to make a career of high school teaching. I had enjoyed the serious work among the teenagers who were "my" enlisted men, but I knew that I needed formal training to make my way into the school systems. Fortunately, I took advantage of credits earned under the G.I. Bill of Rights and enrolled in the Master of Arts in Teaching (MAT) program at Harvard. I had to take an overload of history courses to meet the requirements of the MAT; these courses spurred my interest to carry on in the Graduate School of Arts and Sciences. Shortly after, Nancy, our baby son, and I went to Australia, where I taught history and geography for a year.

When we returned to Harvard University after our year in the Antipodes, I decided to study American history and education, and was lucky to have as my adviser a freshly appointed assistant professor, Bernard Bailyn, who sent me forthwith to the bowels of the Widener Library and into the collected papers of one of the university's greatest presidents, Charles

William Eliot. The president's papers were voluminous, clearly expressed, and frank, and they made for a remarkable story. From these, again at Bailyn's urging and with his help, I wrote a book (*Secondary Schools at the Turn of the Century*), which ultimately was edited and published by the Yale University Press.

While among the Eliot papers, I stumbled across an extraordinary collection of late-nineteenth-century catalogues (advertisements, actually) for the many so-called Academies (more or less secondary schools). Their optimistic goals provided a new window into an understanding of these institutions. A Columbia Teachers College colleague of Bailyn's, Lawrence A. Cremin, asked me to write an analysis of this movement and to select some samples of the catalogues that could paint a fair picture of these little-known institutions, bringing them out of the shadows. I accepted his invitation.

After an introductory essay, I led off with John Milton's 1644 argument, *Of Education,* this followed by Benjamin Franklin's *Proposals Relating to the Youth of Pennsylvania* and the 1778 *Constitution* of Phillips Academy at Andover, Massachusetts. I was inspired by the Academy's very intriguing statement of purpose even then; little did I know then that I would later serve as headmaster of that school. Edward Hitchcock's 1845 *American Academic System Defended* came next, and led me to various catalogues that outlined the rules and regulations at several late-nineteenth-century institutions. The final document, on what the author termed an "altered role" for these kinds of schools, was the National Educational [*sic*] Association's statement "The Place and Functioning of the Academy."

The details and shape of these old institutions need not concern today's educators (save, perhaps, some history teachers who might have an interest in their forebears), but the lesson is clear: schools, then but also now, one by one, should—must—take the time to explain themselves, with jargon-free statements that tell parents and students where they came from, what they stand for, what they do, and why. No educator should feel that he or she is above explaining to "the masses" what he or she is up to, day to day. This is one of the ways in which my scholarship informed both my passion and my career as a teacher and reformer in high school, college, and graduate school.

• • •

Another meaning of *learning* will not appear in the dictionary: the "renewing of your mind." I heard this definition in what public educators might consider an unexpected place—a sermon by the Reverend Peter Gomes at Memorial Church in Cambridge. It nicely suggests that all of us must keep what seems to be important rolling over in our minds, bumping into new shades of meaning depending on the situation. Reverend Gomes helped me see that our learning is not a fixed thing (save for the simple matters: $2 + 2 = 4$), and that, perhaps to our surprise, nonconformity is a virtue.

The use of the mind is the central purpose of schooling. Getting the facts is just the beginning of each person's trek through life, especially because facts are subject to change whenever someone does new and careful research. One must also search for "re-meaning," renewing the understandings that appear apt for our time. "The truth will set us free," Gomes went on, paraphrasing Thomas Jefferson. Citizens in a democracy must be truth seekers, separating the biased or outdated from the defensible and applicable. Teachers (and preachers) must bear witness to this process, modeling for their students what a responsible person in a democracy undertakes. The writing teacher writes stories. The math teacher solves problems far away from his classroom. Gandhi is an example of a modern saint in this context; he heeded the re-meanings that he discovered, to the best of his ability living out what he preached or, better, represented.

• • •

We are supposed to learn in school. Fundamentally, that is what schools are for. In June, each child is expected to know more than he or she did in September. The child learned all that knowledge between late that prior summer and early the succeeding autumn. It is that learning which we teachers hope to facilitate.

We hope that our children will go to school ready to learn, but we must be prepared to be watchful about what they may find there. Some teachers—mercifully not in most current American schools—try to brainwash their citizens of all ages, attracting them to what their leaders want them to know and thereby to act upon. Leaders in Nazi Germany were very adept at this; Hitler appointed Joseph Goebbels as the Reich's propaganda minister—a brilliant choice, as Goebbels was clever, and he knew his various audiences well, including the Jews, many of whom actually believed at first that Hitler's Germany could be trusted, even that the concentration camps into which they were interned were worthy, helpful places. The Nazis persuaded a well-educated and experienced population that what *they* said, and not what anyone else said, was the truth.

From this vantage point decades later, these facts are difficult to accept. However, the evidence is there. Thought control is, to a free people, a cardinal sin. It is dangerous because focused propaganda can be effective. This is why the best teachers insist on a broad range of learning, most especially including skepticism.

We must teach our students to use caution when they are exposed to ideologies that have followers whose enthusiasm clouds their judgment. Politicians understand the use of focused, appealing messages: "If you agree with me on most issues, you should endorse my policies, and you are a fool if you do not." Of course, competing candidates may jump on what they feel are weak or sloppy or likely to be unpopular messages of their opponents. What they call "messages" are points of view that are to be learned so deeply that they compel action, even if the person acting on them is unaware of their source. Leaders want their constituencies to learn these messages well and to be able to sell them to others. "We must march together." In that kind of atmosphere, nuance is considered to be weakness.

Advertisers, too, depend on such "learning." We consumers are aware that they are trying to persuade us, but sometimes they use only part of what is true to leave us with a false impression. Even less salubrious, some persons with one agenda may decide to smear a competitor's messages, making it likely (they hope) that the reader or listener will be gulled into believing what he or she has been told. One sees this at the edges of sales in the advertising community as well as in politics.

If what is being taught in the New American High School is more benign than it was in Nazi Germany—meant to open minds rather than to close them—how do teachers make learning *stick*? That is, how can we be sure that at some future date, what we have taught can be identified, used, and put to work? That's where teachers hope their labors lead. Learning must repeat itself; in a constantly broadening and enriching spiral, our students find new facts and their re-meanings. Or so we hope. This will happen, however, only if we teachers are prepared to accept a paradox: that learning sticks because students are paying attention (or being cajoled into paying attention), but also because they are making connections with other knowledge and other thoughts.

An example will make this point clear. One of our grand-children used to spend the hours in her high school biology class listening, but at the same time practicing her ability to draw the human hand—an activity that greatly distressed her teacher. Because she (the grandchild, not the teacher) is now in medical school, we can see more clearly how the one form of learning was attached to the other, how deeply embedded her attention—and learning—really was. From the beginning of time, most humans surely have daydreamed, their minds seemingly miles away from the rigors of formal instruction, from what a teacher wanted or what a syllabus outlined or what someone with an axe to grind wanted him or her to know. They have often, however, been learning something even more important to them.

Each of us teachers daydreams as well, even as we might deny it to others. Dour, purposeful critics will argue that this isn't the "time on task" for which we are getting paid! In spite of that complaint, good principals, superintendents, and school board members also do such dreaming. Such a dreamer is committed to learning from experience and having the patience to make this skill a habit, or so we hope.

Most of us desire that our political leaders will also be responsible dreamers. From history, we know some who were not, people who did not look ahead in informed and questing ways. They failed to understand what lay ahead for their communities, as well as themselves, and as a result their prescriptions were quickly out-of-date, rigid, and therefore (to their fury) ignored. Worse, they were sometimes followed, and were harmful to those who needed help.

• • •

Learning is about extending some matters of important fact so that they become cogent and usable in a different context and at a different time. We learn on the job, whether we realize it or not. We learn in a number of ways, but we learn best when we are able to practice what we have learned. As we get into a desired routine and find its activities engaging, we learn from that experience and look forward to continuing with it. For example, a student who understands how a pendulum works looks forward to trying it out later in a different setting (such as in the windup of an effective baseball pitcher).

Observers will see this in many middle and high school classes, as the students enjoy explaining to these visitors how what they have constructed works, how and why the pendulum slows down, and what that tells us about moving bodies in space. They are learning a habit that we wish for them: they are coming to be *habitual* learners, or so we have reason to assume. If the process of learning and the useful retention of what that learning is and what it means in a new situation are the residue of what we have taught, we can enjoy some well-deserved satisfaction.

Learning depends on context, but different contexts are appropriate for different students. In fourth grade, our son had a teacher who always insisted on complete quiet in her classroom. She spent much of each day waiting for it, growing more and more frustrated with the few rebels who didn't cooperate. Our son wasn't one of them, but you can imagine his delight when we moved in midyear to England, where his teacher encouraged him to learn math by measuring the dimensions of the classroom and timing his friends' foot races, all recorded in his little notebook. That was where he came to understand the relationship between learning and purposeful activity.

• • •

Learning, of course, goes beyond schools. A novice working in a grocery market learns how to pack a bag with groceries at a checkout station. When she starts, she gets some guidelines from her coworkers: put the heavy, noncrushable items at the bottom and work upward from there, with the frosted birthday cake on top. After that it's practice, practice, practice, and before long she is able to offer guidelines to someone else.

We learn a bit about golf by reading a book on the subject or going to a seminar. The real learning, however, is on an arcade's putting green, learning how to hold the club and understanding why the ball rolls in the way it rolls, the lay of its land. In time, we move up the line to more difficult shots, ultimately to drive off tees.

What we want to learn matters. What other people want us to learn also matters, but not as much. We can say—as I did in eighth grade—"Yes, Mrs. Hitchcock, I 'get' it," while all the time knowing that I hadn't the first idea what she and the text might be telling me. We pretend and hope that she will not call on us or assign a pop quiz. We dodge engagement, but for reasons having nothing to do with "learning" in its most noble sense. Simply, the timing is wrong; we want to learn but are still confused, and thus we fear the humiliation that we would feel if we told her so.

When did fear come to be so dominant in the learning process? When did it come even to prevent learning at some times and for some people? Wise schools make clear to students and parents (and to their new teachers, who are probably themselves thrashing around a bit and trying to hide it) just what it is that their students should know and be able to do. Of course, making such a list is easy. Getting each student to master and make that substance and set of skills his or her own is far more difficult, and for each person a different amount of time, and perhaps a different kind of explanation and sequence, may well be needed. This is obvious to anyone who spends time in classrooms, but too many government education officials who have no or only long-ago experience facing a group of kids from September to June do not appreciate it, to our collective loss.

. . .

Learning is a *process,* not only a pleasurable, useful end in itself. We revere the learned man or woman who knows much and who can apply it. We enjoy increasing what we can do and what we know. The first grader who learns about birds is thrilled to share her new information with her grandparents. She feels that they need to learn what she has to teach, and in our case, she is usually right! She has no fear that she may not know everything. What she knows is more than she used to know, and that gives her enjoyment and a sense of competence.

We teachers often make the mistake of believing (or acting as though we believed) that what was earlier covered was learned—was well, truly, permanently embedded in the student's brain and in his or her conduct. "We thought," we teachers may say, "that you learned that concept/fact/historical happening last year," counting on the hope that what was (presumably) learned earlier somehow has stuck, allowing its use in new and unanticipated situations. "We thought you had learned that you must not horse around in chemistry class; it's too dangerous, as you might break equipment or allow the release of toxic materials." "We hope that you learned—understood—why people turned on John Adams in favor of Thomas Jefferson for president." "We thought that you had learned not to make a sharp turn in your car when traveling at fifty miles per hour."

The process of learning—how we learn, why we learn, when we learn, how different people learn in necessarily different ways—are topics in most university schools of education and in their science laboratories. Anthropologists, for example, study the topic of higher-order mammals, sometimes using primates' simpler processes as a point of entry. High school teachers can act likewise, if they are given class time and administrators' support to teach in this way, toward learning what is useful and what sticks. Too many students, however, only "rent" information—until the test—fully aware of how easy it will be to get it again on the Internet. "Rent the information; own the thinking," they may well believe. Where, however, does one start and the other stop?

• • •

If we are wise, we keep track of how our students' learning develops over a semester or year. Each student will, of course, require a separate record. A sensible school expects such tracking and provides time for the necessary record keeping, including what appears to accelerate that learning and what retards it. Again, we expect no less of our physicians. Their developed craft expects that we are not alike, even from one day to the next, and that they and we must carefully ponder the shape of our illness.

Learning is thought by some to be a chore, but it should be a joy, even a revelation. "Wow," the student says, "I didn't know that!" Both students and teachers seem wary of having too good a time in school, as if enjoying oneself would signify a lack of seriousness. They should put such worries aside, and most learn to as the schoolroom becomes comfortable for them. Effective teachers focus on constructive revelations, one student at a time. Teachers have to start where each child is, to help him or her access as many pieces of data as seems reasonable in that day's context. Traditional textbooks undermine this pattern, as most of them have "one best message." Their style is too often one of exposition rather than of explanation or, better yet, that of a guide for a student's own interpretations. Teachers must pay as little attention as possible to standardized text-driven learning and standardized testing, though this will be a dangerous practice in our day of excessively "sure" cultural and intellectual leaders.

How one organizes assignments and classes can be effective or ineffective prods for learning, depending on the student with whom the teacher is working. Group study and lessons can be constructive if carefully planned; at their best, they engage the students with the reality that all is not necessarily just as they, or their textbook or curricular directions, imply. In groups, students will become familiar with others' learning styles—which are more noisy and interactive, which more silent—and over time will learn more about their own. Some students, however, appreciate ambiguity more than others. Some are more at ease taking criticism or coping with new ideas than other students; a teacher must know which is which and why; she must respect where each student comes from, yet persistently help each one move to a new and more competent place.

Some aspects of learning, like learning the multiplication tables or the scales in music, *are* necessary chores. One plays a simple etude over and over again, finally presenting it to the teacher. Or a budding baseball player shags fly balls until he can catch the ball even while running backward. Much depends on whether the learner really wants to acquire the new skill or is genuinely interested in the subject.

If the teacher or coach feels that work is well done, he or she sets a new, more difficult passage to perform. The player is on a treadmill: as soon as he can do something well, a new, more difficult task is set him. The better one gets, the harder it gets, or so it seems to some frustrated students. "Can't we just stop here?" she asks. "Not if you want to get better and be able to play even more difficult and more rewarding works," her teacher replies. "Imagine what it must be like for a composer as she or he tries to get the idea or sound in your head." Once the musician thinks that the phrase or even the single note is "right," he must then figure out if it works within the chords and passages that were intended. Of course, at some point (we teachers hope) each student "gets it"—by which we mean that he internalizes it—whether it is a fact or something far more fungible.

In this sense, learning is a revelation, something new, unanticipated, as if some daily chore or seemingly mundane occurrence grabbed your attention. In "Stopping in the Woods on a Snowy Evening," a celebrated poem that some may think is simple, elementary school stuff, Robert Frost illumines this love of questing.

This poem reads easily. Most students will "get it," though some may find it mawkish. (They won't use that word; indeed, they might not know that it exists.) The poem makes something important—educational—of a seemingly humble matter such as a single snowflake or the rustle of leaves or the property of another. It hints at subtle communication between man and beast. Simple though it may first appear, there is much here into which a student can and must dig; each student must learn to respect such worthy intellectual activity, as it rests at the core of serious scholarship.

Imagination, too, plays a role. Some students might see something in an issue that has eluded even you, their teacher, such as the deliberate *mis*use of standard punctuation and capitalization in the reading of a T. S. Eliot poem. This sort of analysis—this sort of learning—involves hard intellectual work, including the work of tuning the ear in singing or in a play with words, or the ability to discern an unusual word order, words that carry some special meaning that can become rewarding. A wise teacher can make use of such an exercise for several classes and can swing back to it even some months later.

• • •

Finally, what is learned can be good or bad.

One can learn that when you make funny faces at little children in subways, they seem to enjoy it, but when you stare at the face of the adult traveler across the narrow aisle from you to while away the time, his face will get deliciously red. The more that traveler shows anger, the more fun it is to provoke him, fun that is actually impolite, but at times irresistible. You are learning, but is that learning useful?

To be useful, learning must have a worthy purpose and become a *habit*. A trip down this road starts with the questions "Why?" "How?" and "What?"—the major interrogatives in the English language. A wise person asks these questions virtually without thinking; a wise teacher guides his students to acquire the habit of asking them.

Such questions include, "Just what was it that that politician said? Was she being serious, or was she merely trying to get my attention?" or "For what reason was my colleague asking me that question? Is there a specific objective hidden behind that query?"

One can be curious or skeptical without being rude, but one has to keep an eye on just how the intended listener is reacting. Especially in a classroom of young or sensitive students, a teacher has to be careful. She can ask a question in a way that seems demanding but useful to her, but that might have the effect of putting down—thereby publicly humiliating—a student. This switches the student's mind from a genuine intellectual quest to an emotional disappointment, and defeats the purpose, then and possibly later.

A good question in one context may be a bad question in another. For example, why did we join in the fight against Nazism? Does even asking such a question imply that we have made the wrong choice? Does asking for reasons imply that some are better than others? *Are* some reasons better than others? There are many answers, ranging from "It was our moral duty to stand against those who would assault people such as the Jews" to "It was fundamentally self-defense, if not now, then later." We can assign value to each of these responses, which may guide us in making future decisions like this one. Or if we are interested in the Germans' motives as well as our own, we may ask, "What do we make of Germans who opposed Hitler, at risk of their lives?"

Sometimes we must rely on what others have learned. Candidates for public office must communicate without being able to see the effects on their listeners, especially if they are speaking to television cameras or a radio microphone. Their aides interview citizens who share demographics to determine what these hearers and watchers sense; they then advise and drill the candidate on what they believe that they have learned. Both candidates and aides then pray that their research and judgment hold up. Competitive businesses do likewise, hiring consultants to try out ideas—even individual words—on various focus groups.

• • •

All these observations about learning have several important implications for education policy and practice. Of course these implications will vary from one target group to another, depending on the likely area from which each comes; and how a single teacher's 9:00 AM seventh-grade class behaves might be quite different from the way the same students react to demanding questions in a 2:15 PM class with another teacher. There are two important variables here, and often both the students and the teachers grow weary and restless just before the school day is over.

There is more to it than that, however. Even if the time, the teacher, and the students were the same, the subtlety required in school teaching highlights the need for a very savvy instructor who can discern much from something as banal as the slouch of a particular student who usually is erect or even leaning forward trying to get the teacher's attention in an annoying way. Again, teaching, at its best, is a subtle art, and that is why our profession is so attractive and engaging to many of us.

These obvious realities affect teacher education. Beginning teachers have to build up the habit and a repertoire of ways of sensing the mood of an entire class or that of a single student, mood having much to do with each individual's learning. The teacher can sample the overall mood (if, in fact, there is one)—that is, the readiness of the class to settle down. The unpredictability of some responses will inevitably put a teacher on her toes. She might have planned ahead for the possible reactions of her early (say, 9:45 AM) class and those for the one after lunch; the eyes will usually be brighter in the former than in the latter, but this may be the day when a topic is unusually compelling, when the desire to learn becomes more powerful than the disadvantages in the learning environment.

There is mystery in learning. Even the learner may be surprised at what he thought was a good answer or analysis at one point and that he later dismisses as being dull and not revealing of what he means. The unpredictability makes teaching interesting and makes learning interesting for a student of any age. How *boring* it would be if you got the exact response you wanted from every child every time. Indeed, longtime teachers who still take delight in their craft are pleased when they are surprised, when their students have expanded the teachers' own horizons and their own learning, while they are at the same time able to separate the wheat from the chaff.

CHAPTER · FOUR

Differences

No two of us are alike. No one of us stays the same, day to day.

Of course we differ, and thank goodness we do. How boring it would be if we were clones. Even the sour kid in the back row of my classroom who stares at the ceiling makes the day interesting. His glower is fun to watch. It changes as the period proceeds; he stares rudely at the classmate who answers my query accurately. Is it jealousy or disdain? As the lunch break approaches, he may even show a slight smile.

Some animals and birds that we observe appear to us to be alike, indistinguishable. Yet many of those animals have particular mates to whom they are and remain devoted. The squirrels that dominate our bird feeders appear to be alike, clones even, yet when we watch them carefully, there appear to be slight but important differences among these feisty rodents. One of them tries endlessly to tackle the feeders by getting atop the roof of our house, peering carefully and then leaping down on one of our cylindrical feeders. He or she rarely makes contact, but the creature's hope—and hunger—spring eternal.

Another has discovered that a window screen that is near to all those seeds can be used as a sort of staircase to the cache. He leaps at the screen, making quite a noise, and quickly climbs toward dinner. These two squirrels appear identical, but in their actions they appear to be not quite the same. The biblical story of the march of animals two by two arises from a false, albeit understandable, belief.

Most of us (and, who knows, maybe even squirrels) at some point ask the solemn question, "Who am I? Why am I here, on this earth? What makes me special, a unique person unlike any other here now or living in the past?" My aunts tell me that I look just like my father, without the mustache. Sure, I know that. I have brown eyes and hair, and he had brown eyes and hair (until the latter turned white, as have my locks, such that remain after chemotherapy for cancer). Our elder son, Theodore Sizer II, has a mustache like my father, but his blue eyes appear to have been borrowed from Nancy's father, Harold Eimer Faust.

Identity and *diversity* are fighting words these days. If I look different from everyone else, does that mean that I should be treated differently? Turn off the lights, I say, and then figure out how different the two of us are. Sure, you're a girl and I'm a boy, but we both have the ability to laugh. When I am hurt in an accident and have lost quite a bit of blood, I can get a transfusion from almost anyone, unless they have a blood disease or a comparable condition such as cancer.

The concepts of diversity and identity are related in a variety of ways. Diversity cannot happen in the absence of clearly defined identities. Unless we know the general parameters of a person's *identity* (an individual's particular characteristics), we cannot describe—and ultimately make use of—a *diverse* human population such as the students in many American high schools, especially those that draw students from a variety of communities.

Differences are *interesting*. Does any imaginative teacher want to instruct classes of students who learn in exactly the same way? Most of us like the intellectual banging of one kid's mind against that of another—and against our own. Successful teachers are cocky, in the best sense. Alas, some of us find this jousting threatening, fearing that the class will get out of control—meaning that noise will attract the attention of administrators patrolling the school's halls.

Teachers also often worry about the quiet ones, the students who are sometimes labeled "mousy nerds." Why are they silent? Are they like mice, frightened and trying to hide in a corner, not moving so as to avoid anyone's noticing that they are present? Are they intimidated by their noisy peers? Are they afraid that they might be mocked by the other students and even by you, the teacher? "Oh, Jamie," you might say, "can't you *ever* see something apart from your obsession with horses?" The reproach may seem gentle to you, even signaling that you know Jamie and her passions well. Jamie, however, may not see it that way, and she will shrink behind her desk. Is this kind of teasing acceptable in a classroom? Can your unintended slight be undone? Forgiven, and not only by

Jamie? Or perhaps the class is quiet just because that is who they are; it is part of their collective personality.

We are born with some differences: gender, race, social class, even some aspects of our personalities. Personalities, however, can evolve. Can each of us, you or I or any teenager, decide what our identity is and insist that all others respect and honor it? For example, can I choose to be a heroic kind of guy?

More seriously, can a teenager learn deeply and well if he or she lacks the self-confidence that ideally arises from self-knowledge? Serious learning is hard work, so if her identity is as a nonlearner, to her at least, she is all too likely to give up far too soon. She might still be a star on the field hockey team, but the confidence arising from such happy notoriety will not automatically help her learn history easily. Identity is fungible; it changes as new experiences affect it.

When I was young, I was aware of my identity: youngest, brown-eyed, and above all, boy, but more attributes were about to be added, among them my self-perception of being dumb. I was sent to school early, but was no superstar there. Thus I was, with my mother and two of my sisters, in what the family called the "Dumb Club"; my father and three other sisters, including Alice, were in the "Bright Club." All this was supposed to be a joke, but it never struck me that way. My mother put herself into the Dumb category to support us; she was hardly ever dumb by any definition. To be sure, after being "finished" at Miss Porter's School in Farmington, Connecticut, she, like the overwhelming majority of young women of her social class and generation, did not go to college. Instead, like her sisters, she "came out" into society and came home to the Boston Sewing Circle, which offered her company and a gentle workshop in that craft. In those days, it was thought that too much schooling for women might make them annoyingly opinionated and less willing to become happy homemakers and the producers of children, or, if unmarried, someone who would willingly staff the family business or farm, take it over when needed, and willingly take over the care of the parents when they grew old.

By the time I was assigned to the Dumb Club, my mother's obvious competence and managerial brilliance were in full flower. She kept the family's financial books and its calendar, made most of the household decisions and undertook all, or nearly all, of the family's most intricate interpersonal challenges. So her example, which reminded me and two of my sisters that school-smarts were not the only important qualifications for a well-led life, may have been intended to offer us some solace. One thing I am sure of is that she never intended to hurt us. For all I know, my sisters may even have thought it *was* funny. Still, for me at least, and surely for most others at any time, it was not fun to be called dumb. My own academic work in elementary and middle school showed that the label of dumbness could be a corrupting, self-fulfilling prophecy. The way I saw it, if all those smart people—my parents included—think that I am dumb, then I must be dumb.

Alas, such cruel prophecies still exist among us. In too many bureaucratic and political quarters, a child from a low-income or immigrant family, or, in some communities, a girl, must be dumb. Insisting that differentiation is the best way to enable solid learning and that children must be described so that teachers can create practical lesson plans, teachers try to make their challenging and complex task simpler. Parents, especially those of academically precocious students, tend to go along with it. Yet people who do such labeling are, in fact, cruel, even as they may believe that categorizing each child, usually on the basis of multiple-choice, standardized, timed tests, is an act of charity. "It is better that she is with her own kind," they might say. "That way she won't get discouraged. We have special sections for her."

So tracking abounds. In large high schools, those in the top tracks may never cross paths with their academic "inferiors." At the same time, diversity has become a desired and clearly articulated goal in education today, the justification being that we must learn to get along with people from races or ethnic groups or religions—even genders, in this supposedly sophisticated age—different from ours. Further, being in a school classroom of clones is likely to be intellectually stifling. Variety, at least in the hands of skillful teachers, is an effective prod for deeper learning.

How can teachers respond to these contradictory messages and conditions? Many of us today believe that students must mix it up, each young scholar arguing a proposition that might usefully clash with or connect to another. This would blunt the effect of categorizing students and instead reach out to the separate imagination in each young person's mind. A middle school teacher might create a debate topic—say, "Keep It Clean"—and divide the class into teams. Time would be given for each team to figure out what "keeping it clean" meant (Thoroughly washed? Clear of drugs?) and decide on a debate strategy, eventually assigning roles to each of its members. Teachers would insist that every student play a part, not just the adept debaters. Inclusive assignments would be necessary if the entire class were to engage with the topic and thus to learn.

Some might say that this tactic is a waste of time, slowing down the march toward greater knowledge by focusing on one homely term such as *cleanliness*. That argument is just backward: the teacher is trying to develop in each youngster's mind the need for clarity and precision in the use of language, even specific words.

"Remember the *Maine!*" is a good example of a hook on which to catch and hold a youngster's attention, fixing young minds on the Spanish-American War and the destruction of that prized American warship. It will also (we teachers hope) introduce and usefully fix in each student's mind the concept of a surprise assault on a major warship, from Cuba to Pearl Harbor. Because it was also a slogan, one never supported with facts about how (or by whom) it actually blew up, it is another example of the need for precision in language, the need for each young mind to become a careful crap detector. Discussions about peremptory strikes and their place in warfare and other arenas will reveal much about differences of opinion and how they are justified.

The New Deal is an example of another hook, here fixing the pupil's attention and memory on President Franklin D. Roosevelt's characterization of the legislative proposals that he sent to the Congress. The teacher could ask, Why was that compact new? Was it an extension of the earlier Progressive

Era? What did the president mean by "Deal"? Deal between whom and whom? The market and the people who have been harmed by it? The government and the people whom it is meant to protect? Is the concept of "deal" a usefully generic one? How do today's slogans sell? What aspects of a person's experience and values are they meant to awaken? When is an emotional reaction useful in helping a person think more clearly?

Besides general discussions like these, how can adults teach specifically toward identity? That is, how can we teach each student to shape and respect what is ever emerging in his or her sense of himself or herself? When a young person is developing his own ethical code—what he would do or would never do—are those decisions based on emotional revulsion or consistent principles?

Some suggestions for helping students come to grips with their own uniqueness:

- Ask students to write short autobiographies, these framed in terms of incidents in their lives that—they now realize—carry meanings in ways they had not earlier considered. "Oh, that's not *me*!" a student might say. You respond, "*How* is it not *you*?" And "What is meant by the concept of *meaning* to you as an individual?" If a student is a weak writer, ask her to start with a diagram or to sketch a picture that displays what she feels and understands. Draw examples from literature, you ask, where a key character provides an image of a sort of person. Or use classics that depend for their meaning on a character—Huck Finn, for example, or Romeo and Juliet—individuals who represent a way of life or a set of beliefs but who also had strong ties to their communities.

- Turn to history: What made and yet makes Israel a *homeland* for Jews, a place that represents who many of them are and what they stand for? Indeed, just what is a home, much less a homeland, and who decides? Or study the tribes of Nigeria, such as the Ibos and Hausas. Why did these separate cultures evolve, and why have they persisted over centuries in shaping each person's identity? When have these identities been shed, at least temporarily? What can be learned from these examples?

- Make use of current events to sharpen the notion and importance of identity. Ask students to study the published materials from a political candidate's campaign, materials that were most likely crafted by staff members and then handed to the candidate to read. Suggest that students watch any televised debates that might be aired in an election cycle. How did John McCain position himself in the 2008 presidential campaign? Why did his handlers decide to limn that image? How did Hillary Clinton separate herself from Barack Obama in that campaign? What difference might it have made? How, in 20-20 hindsight, did those images work? What does "work" mean in this situation? How do individual personalities affect democracy? Most social studies classes will come alive with this sort of discussion.

- In biology or animal behavior class, study how animals other than humans shape their turf and define themselves. Visit a Doggie School, where dogs are trained to perform all sorts of tasks, ranging from being housebroken to learning to serve as the eyes of a blind person. A guide dog has an identity, easily perceived, loyalty being at the heart of it.

- Eventually, assign each student to illumine the concept of identity with an example, whether found in fiction, past reality, today's reality, or even his or her own experience.

All this time-consuming schoolwork is important because it represents the practice of introspection and the often hurtful practice of labeling people, whether siblings or figures that emerge in current events classes. How one sees oneself and how one registers what one sees in others is important learning.

There will be diversity here. We meet and have to work with others different from ourselves. As individuals, we grow older; our identity when we are twenty-seven will not be precisely the same as when we are sixty-seven. We change as our lives change. Some wits tell us that long marriages make wife and husband ever more alike. This is no surprise; common activity affects choices, habits, and attitudes. We meld identities.

Finally, get the students into the habit of looking in the mirror, asking questions about just whom they see. Do I *respect* that person I see? Do I *like* that person I see? What new things can and should that new person do? What old habits must be shed?

Is all this identity stuff appropriate work for schools? Shouldn't this delicate matter be left to family members? Isn't our concern about each child's identity an invasion of that young person's privacy? No, as long as we are sensitive to where, with a particular student, we may go too far.

• • •

All this may appear to a student (or a teacher) to be far-fetched. Are studies of words or phrases what education should, at least to some degree, be about? The answer is yes. People associate themselves with convictions (expressed by a word or a small collection of words) that, almost without their thinking, become useful labels for ideas and opinions that provide each individual with a useful shorthand. "She's an *activist.*" "He's a *ball of fire.*" "They are a *piece of work.*" "He runs like a *three-legged donkey.*"

This argument for self-conscious identity formation connects with a parallel goal for diversity. The two beliefs are two sides of the same coin. The concept of identity can serve as a caution, such as "Beware the salesman who brings you simplistic slogans like 'large is good and small is bad.'" If that marketer gives you only a single image, he distorts reality. Young people should be made well aware of this sort of distortion, as their world is full of sales pitches pouring in from every quarter.

At the same time, a catchy identity can serve as a simple, useful device for memorizing—deliberately or unintentionally—a fact or event around which other events can connect.

It simplifies both the teacher's and the students' job. The government activity and legislation in the 1930s was varied and complex, expensive, and often at cross-purposes with itself, yet teachers may counsel their students to "Remember this label—the New Deal—and you will do well on the upcoming state tests," particularly if the tests are little more than questions about currently popular facts.

Labels can also be applied to students, with unfortunate but also beneficial results. Gathering kindling with my young grandson, I find I must answer his question, "Am I good at this?" Behind his question is, of course, "Am I better than my brothers?" It will do neither of us any good to try to devise a measurement system for gathering kindling, so I tell him that he's the most enthusiastic gatherer I have seen in quite some days. That seems to please—even to inspire—him, and in fact his productivity is impressive. A teacher, too, might ask, *How might this conception influence each student's sense of self?* "This is who I am!" "I am a doer." "I am a careful person." "I am a failure." "I hate all this, and you too." These are strong labels, ones that can cut two ways, one hurtful, the other supportive.

Neither a teacher nor a parent wants a child to describe himself or herself in a narrow, suffocating way, but the practice of close definition—creating a pigeonhole, if you will—is an effective exercise. Using the arts and literature is a good device to make points about identity in a manner that is separate from each student's own sense of self, yet contributes to its development. The nature of a character in literature, or a portrait of a person in the sciences—say, of J. Robert

Oppenheimer—keeps the matter at arm's length while still conveying what it is to be someone.

With all humility, we teachers and school designers must face up to the fact that having different youngsters, each with a separate personality and readiness to learn, forces our hands: we have to accommodate that complexity. We cannot avoid it. Most students pay attention to us at least some of the time, especially as we come up against both their differences and our desire to treat each one fairly. Nancy and I experienced this prickly reality in our teaching, and we used it in the title of our book on moral education: *The Students Are Watching: Schools and the Moral Contract*. The happy sales figures of that book suggest that we hit a widely recognized nerve. Most parents and teachers know all too well that the children in their lives are observing them.

Matters of identity are not confined to schools. Many age mates as well as students of ours gossip about us behind our backs or where they may think our backs are; most of us teachers can recall hearing about just who we are, without the teenagers' awareness that we are within hearing. Widely available magazines are a further indication of our interest in and often obsession with other folk, *People* being a prime example.

I have been labeled within my hearing (especially when I was a principal) as both "soft" and "hard," as "strict" or a nice and readily manipulated "pushover." In time I found all this more humorous than painful. Nancy would tease me about some students' beliefs about my character. She would say, "If those kids only knew . . ." I usually was glad that they did not.

We teachers cannot dodge identity development even if we wanted to. Our students morph before us even if we want no part of all that morphing. What's more, their Facebook entries show that they are recording all these changes with or without our help. We must accept this challenge and live with its pressures and complexities. Differences count.

Just as we teachers come to recognize the value in our students' different opinions, we must also be ready to teach them in a variety of ways. If, in the style of John Dewey, the child is truly to be at the center of her own education, we must be prepared to address her in several fashions: visual, auditory, kinesthetic, but even more. We must know whether a slower or quicker pace, a brisk or loving style, a competitive or collaborative model, will lead to the best outcomes for each particular activity. Even if we decide that a particular child learns best by hearing things, we must be prepared to explain those things in several ways, as many as it takes; hearing is not enough.

This teaching style is particularly important in math and science, where so many children feel left behind. The second or third explanation is often the one that works, though too many children are never offered it. Or if the student is a visual learner, we can add pictures and graphs to her fare. More hands-on learners will collect water samples and test them. This more effective and just form of differentiation does not need to reduce one's curriculum or lower one's standards. It may take longer, but schools are not assembly lines because children are not widgets.

• • •

So where does all this play into the design of a *New* American High School? And how can policymakers help students achieve these worthy goals?

They can design schools so that no teacher has more students than she or he can get to know well, a smaller number for beginning professionals and a larger number for the veterans. To teach different children well without categorizing them unfairly, you must be able to know them, and you cannot know each student well if your load is, say, 180 children. Many will state that a smaller ratio—say, eighty to one—is unobtainable. That would indeed be the case if their high school continued to provide a wide variety of offerings. However, they can keep each school small, or, in a large school, keep each house (or whatever term seems relevant in a particular situation) small, maybe three hundred students in a 7–12 school and a similar number for a house unit within a large school. By Thanksgiving, most of the students will know most of their peers, to some extent. Familiarity with their surroundings will lead to a sense of safety that will enhance learning.

Policymakers must allow—indeed must encourage—teachers to assess students in a variety of ways. There must be visible authenticity in the assessment, so that each child sees its usefulness and can explain her work to others. There must be many chances to get feedback and revise, until each student learns to self-assess and self-edit with ever less help. The importance of the assessment will be recognized, but the high-stakes frenetic atmosphere, tense and supercharged, which so disables some students, must not be allowed to get out of control. Fear may make people study, but it rarely leads to lasting learning. The student may often remember the fear but not the material that he was being asked to understand and remember.

When a student's mastery of the material seems secure, promote her on the basis of her exhibited performance, both written and oral. This promotion may be moving her to work with a different group of students, or it may just mean that once a student has shown that she can do a certain kind of work, you move her to new and more challenging work. Check regularly to see if your earlier judgments were on the mark. Solicit the opinions of other teachers who have her in their classes now or had her as a pupil in a preceding year. Keep things flexible. Don't too quickly pigeonhole a student, either in your mind or in assignments, to a fixed, stereotypical category. Always keep your mind open; she may change in front of your eyes, and you must adapt to that change.

We educators must help each child, one by one, find out—however tentatively—who he is, what makes life interesting (in the best sense). This is sensitive work, requiring that teachers know their students well, recalculating their judgments as the adolescents grow up. The fourteen-year-old I taught before is rarely today's seventeen-year-old. Certainly much is the same, but the differences bear attention. Deciding who Joe is when he is fourteen and assuming three years later that we have before us precisely the same Joe is a mistake. School faculties must have good memories of each child to pass along to new teachers, but, because to be human is to evolve, especially in a new context and a new relationship, the old impressions must be discarded when new ones are made.

Teachers must do as well by each individual as the best of physicians do by their patients. I have seen the bulging folder kept by my doctors pass from one to the next, and I have waited patiently as each reviewed what needed to be freshly examined. I have been grateful when, realizing that one strategy was not working, they changed to another one—without blaming me. Often doctors have asked me questions: "What were we worrying about last October? I have forgotten the details." They make no apologies for "forgetting"—if they had, I would have been concerned—but they want those details all the same. My oncologist has all my records on a small computer, and we and Nancy look over the files together. Students deserve such personal attention to details.

• • •

So what does this identity business—the recognition of differences—have to do with schooling? Should each student be on a search for his or her identity? Yes, of course; whether we like it or not, each child is searching. "I *am* somebody" is what each of us, of every age, wants. We want to be special, unique; how we hate to hear from doting relatives or longtime friends of our family that we are "just like your older sister when she was your age." We are torn between, on the one hand, the comfort of family and of wearing the same kinds of blue jeans as our friends wear, and, on the other hand, the desire to be a distinctive individual. We feel confused, even buffeted, as some families and schools in effect pull us close and at the same time push us in the opposite direction. We feel the twin attractions of loyalty to those who have been good to us and a desire to explore the excitement and gratification of thinking for ourselves. This is a lifelong quest—to find the place in which community and individuality can coexist—but it is also a reasonable goal for each of us. In our high school, we must be prepared to help each of our students in this difficult undertaking.

CHAPTER · FIVE

The Language of Schooling

Words count. They can clarify an idea and situate it in time or place.

They can provoke objection. "Don't call me that awful name!" "Don't remind me of the time I failed that exam!"

Words are the necessary language of all bureaucracies, and schools are, willy-nilly, bureaucracies. Words shape the way we think, and control the vocabulary of our work. The language of schooling is influential. Often the words indicate the kind of behavior that is expected.

"First bell." This marks the opening of the school day. Everyone is supposed to quiet down and head for the expected classroom. When students and teacher arrive there, everyone is supposed to settle down. If there is too much chatting, a confident teacher may tell the class to be silent, "respectful" of the task at hand. (A student teacher may not know what to do—to speak or not to speak? and what kind of language to use? Yet if she is silent—or, worse, ineffectual—the noise may even increase.)

"Lunch for eighth graders."

"The whistle blew."

"The principal is the head teacher."

Such expressions are familiar to virtually every school person and most parents and guardians as well.

In most schools, your age is another word, and how old you are counts. *Age* is a word with very specific meaning: a length of time; exactly how many days you have lived on this earth. Not where you have lived or what your experiences have been, but the single, measurable criterion. We call a seventh grader a *child,* and he will snort in response. "I am *not* a child. Give me a break!" You may gently reply, "If you are not a child, what are you? Have you no parents?" All this with a smile. That response may slow him down, given his likely annoyance, and he may well respond, "Come on." By reminding him of his age at a time when he probably wishes that he were older, twenty instead of twelve, you have distracted him. Perhaps you have even changed his behavior.

Some words—*vindication,* for example—imply a sort of selfishness. "Thorn in one's side" can imply keeping a dicey issue at the top of a school's agenda when most of the staff would like the issue to disappear. The practice of democracy—another word loaded with significance—would usually honor the majority in this case, but it is also true that most schools often need such a thorn. Dodging an issue is no solution. Indeed, it may make things worse.

Words fill and circumscribe places for learning. We talk about schools as though they were merely constructed places, buildings, masonry and lumber crafted into spaces where "classes" are held. Within these places, we offer "programs," each made up of a number of "courses." Each of these courses, if successfully completed, add up to a "year" of work, this year usually described in term of "credits." The whole system is mechanical, seemingly designed by people more concerned with dependable uniformity than service for those of us at the bottom of the bureaucratic pyramid. Familiar words can be helpful guideposts, but too many people consider them hitching posts.

As a writer, I know that words can convey all sorts of meaning. I could have titled this book *Today's American High School,* and readers may have expected a description and, perhaps, a critique of the status quo. However, adding the single, familiar word "new"—*The* New *American High School*— deliberately aimed its orientation toward the future. That is, an added word, or a rearrangement of words, will inevitably shape the way a person or a policy is perceived.

• • •

Nearly three decades ago, I and several colleagues were granted generous funds by the Carnegie Corporation of New York to look carefully at the American secondary schools of those years, the 1980s. We called our inquiries a Study of High Schools. Three books—bushels of language!—emerged from that effort, and the volumes' titles were chosen to summarize our findings.

Arthur Powell, Eleanor Farrar, and David Cohen and several assistants carefully and systematically observed sixteen secondary schools across the country, most them public, some nonpublic, and several church-related. Their book's contents were aptly summarized in the title they chose: *The Shopping Mall High School: Winners and Losers in the Educational Marketplace.*

Such a school, they explained, is a place that an adolescent attends for up to ten months per year, moving ahead on the basis of his or her age unless notably floundering; and in that troubling event, the young person is labeled as one with "special needs." This occurs as if most American teenagers had no "special" needs; I cannot think of any such "needs-less" young person. Our children are special, one by one; they— even twins, as I know from my own grandchildren—are not clones.

These young scholars, no matter what their individual interests might be, are usually provided with a few "core" courses—English, mathematics, science, and social studies, and, in some schools in wealthier school districts, foreign language (usually Spanish, with French and German available as electives). Well-funded districts provide the students with "electives," each usually a semester or a year in length, often in the fine and performing arts. The word *core* is itself instructive—as the term is used in schools, the core makes up the central part, the most important and "required" courses. Teachers of "core subjects" are the royalty of a school's faculty. Courses outside this core are nice but not necessary. New teachers like the protection that being in the core provides them.

Despite the greater status of the core courses, in *The Shopping Mall High School*, all the high school's courses were compared to "shops" in the mall, and many electives were offered as much credit as the core courses. One way or another, each student assembled a "program" of courses, few of which had been planned by a specific school's faculty members in relationship to one another. That is, the students browsed among the offerings (the stuff at the mall), from a catalogue or by sitting in on some classes. Many checked out which of their colleagues might be in their classes ("I want Susie in my class!"), when those classes met ("No 8 AM classes for me!"), and who was likely to teach them ("Watch out for Old Man Smith; he's a tough grader, and he throws chalk at kids when he believes they are daydreaming").

The portrait that Powell, Farrar, and Cohen painted was of high school as a sort of mindless bazaar, with young people wandering among the offerings and selecting those that appeared most worthy, interesting, or easiest. Overall, the authors' picture of students as academic consumers was not a pretty one. The scene they described, however, was a persuasive, powerfully argued American embarrassment (as many of the book's reviewers agreed), and so it continues to be.

In another book in our series, Robert Hampel took on the task of writing the history of the twentieth-century secondary school. Rather than visiting many institutions, Hampel looked at the records of a variety of secondary schools, public and private, large and small. His task for the study was carefully limited to put our current schools into the context from which they arose. He chose as his book's title *The Last Little Citadel*, an image of high school as the ultimate place where most young Americans received an education. Social class counted, obviously; wealthier adolescents had more choices for study beyond secondary school graduation. Ironically, the young people who most needed a formal education—children from low-income or otherwise chaotic homes—usually received less of it, thereby extending the gap between poorer children and financially secure or intact middle-class families.

My summary volume was titled *Horace's Compromise: The Dilemma of the American High School*; it embodied what I had absorbed from the extensive field notes produced by my colleagues and also what I had seen and heard in visits to over forty secondary schools across the country, from Boston to Baltimore to Shasta (California) to Broken Bow and Ansley, Nebraska, to Fort Worth, Texas. At some places, I sought out education reporters from local newspapers and gathered from them their sense of what was a "good" or "not-so-good" high school. My wife, Nancy, and I together looked at the San Domenico School in San Anselmo, California, and high schools in Redmond and Marin County. I presented my initial findings at the annual national meetings of the National Association of Secondary School Principals and the National Association of Independent Schools; these two organizations had publicly sponsored the study's work and opened doors that might otherwise have remained shut. At these gatherings, I got strong and useful feedback and quickly gained a sense of how and what our school colleagues thought about our conclusions.

• • •

Over time, I have become intensely sensitive to the words we used then and that I use now, to the way that we talk about schools and the attitudes that this talk—and the talk of others—appears to represent. No phrase used these days has more tightly gripped Americans than the title of the signature piece of early-twenty-first-century federal legislation, the No Child Left Behind Act.

The implications here, both cosmic and specific, are obvious. *Of course* no child—our kin or the kin of others, even the offspring of total strangers—should be excluded from our concern, that is, left behind, discarded, or neglected. The sentiment is almost banal in its obviousness, especially in a modern, wealthy democracy.

NCLB implies nothing in its title about who the potentially "left behind" might be or what specifically we should do about them, considering the tight meaning signaled, say, by most state and federal civil rights legislation. Yet in its over one thousand pages, the law outlined procedures that exhibited a kind of contempt for the "underserved" schools it was meant to help.

• • •

Most of our school systems, public and nonpublic, are deliberately specific in their selectivity ("You cannot enroll here unless you live in our district"). Yet thanks to the long history of local control in most states, educators and school boards have running room to do much as they want. They may complain about being tied up in someone else's objectives, but they—we—have great flexibility and scope for our work. Thus a "*New* American High School" is not just a cluster of nice words but an opportunity and a complex challenge. We know that what we Americans have all around us does not function well, does not live up to its rhetorical promise, and begs attention.

What more cogent words and phrases should dominate our conversations and thoughts about schools and their design? Language is important, as it captures and inevitably guides our thinking about what a "new" sort of school might be. That said, language—words—morph over time. What was precise usage in the 1920s may not make much sense today.

The following are some possible candidates for words to guide our thinking and planning, the first in Latin:

Cogito ergo sum. I think, therefore I am. Try though a human may, he or she cannot stop the intellectual churning. Even when we shut our eyes, the ideas continue gushing forth. *What am I going to do tomorrow? What did he mean when he said that? Why did he say it?* We cannot escape our own thinking, even when we try to, such as when we fail to fall asleep prior to an important day ahead. In what ways should we capitalize on this human trait by giving students more practice and variety in thinking?

Public. We want the programs that protect us—police and fire services especially—to be planned and directed by people whom we elect to do that overseeing. We want such services extended equally to all. We do not want some outside group marching in and telling us that its special and thus likely narrow and "gated" community will increase safety for the community as a whole. We define what is "public," usually self-consciously, even as we understand that private institutions also frequently serve a public good.

School. This is the word that Americans have long chosen to denote the place where people gather in order to teach and learn. Sometimes we qualify it with identification as an elementary school, a middle or junior or senior high school, a graduate school of arts and sciences, a law school, and so on—defined as a place where people gather for some stated purpose, such as in marine studies, where there will be reference to a *school* of fish. In one exercise in Nancy's and my recent class at Harvard, however, we asked the students to use the word "school" as a verb rather than a noun. The exercise caused no end of discomfiture at first, but made its point: schooling is primarily a process. It involves learning, but goes even further than learning. "Well-schooled" has a specific meaning, involving certain kinds of skills and knowledge.

Growth. We want our children to grow, in the positive sense of that word. We want them to know about things and objects within their sight and hearing. We should be explicit about what we mean: growth in what we consider to be a positive direction, one that we could defend in the face of potentially hostile critics. We wish children to become responsible adults, in the traditional sense of personal responsibility and order and a respect for others. All this implies self-restraint.

Awareness. We want our young people to be vigilant, watchful, taking in what they see and hear and feel and making sense of it all. This end affects the way we conduct our schools (and our homes, streets, and more). What do our students see and hear in these different venues? What value do they put on this experience? Everything we do in schools is inevitably seen and heard by most everyone of every age in a school building.

We expect our students to be aware, and dissecting a frog in a biology lab, analyzing religion in history class, and discussing suicide in English all increase that awareness. At the same time, we must introduce these experiences at the right time, and understand that what we do and what everyone else does in this intensively populated school building affects most of everything else.

Habit. Ultimately we want our students to exhibit the thoughtful use of what they hear, feel, and observe in the world around them. This is "taught" mostly by modeling it ourselves. "Good" habits—for both teachers and students— mean that we do the right thing when no one is looking, which implies that we are internally sensitive to our impact on the immediate environment around us.

Understanding. By this we mean "to know something thoroughly," by which we mean something mastered deeply enough to use in new contexts. If an adolescent cannot use these new learnings in important and relevant situations, he or she has not truly mastered them. To stress again: the ultimate purpose of education is to develop the ability to *understand* important matters well and to *use* those matters for worthwhile personal and social ends.

Why, in the sense of the asking of questions, especially if through such asking, a student learns to be inquisitive about something of importance. "Why did Grant and Lee decide to stop fighting and to start negotiating when they did to end the Civil War?" Why then, at that moment, and not earlier or later? Why did they think—finally—that there might be middle ground between the Union and Confederate sides on which to build the beginning of a stable peace?

Why did these two men trust each other? That trust saved this nation.

Maturation. This word—and the idea it reflects—carries with it a value-laden sense of what a mature person is or should endeavor to be. It is a variant of *growth,* but implies a different sort of process, one that has to do with a young person's ability to make wise, or at least principled, choices. We need not agree with all of our adolescents' emerging ideas; it is in the nature of youthful generations to be skeptical of their elders, and conditions in the neighborhood or in the larger world are in inevitable movement. "Mother, how *could* you believe that!" Mother has to keep her temper.

Freedom. This is a familiar American word, but one that we all too frequently apply primarily to ourselves. "I want and deserve freedom, but those sloppy authorities across town do not deserve it. Some of them are socialists! Their license weakens the freedom that the rest of us enjoy." Free minds are necessary for the functioning of democracy, however turbulent it might be. Of course, most teenagers glory in their perceived "freedom," finding its possibilities almost endless.

Restraint. This is a word with good and bad connotations. Restraining oneself from talking so that others may be heard is simple politeness. Restraining someone from speaking in order to prevent that person's ideas from being heard is, in all but extreme cases, inappropriate. Restraining a person in, say, a straitjacket, can be either good or bad—good if the person is likely to hurt himself and others if not checked, and bad if one is merely trying to shut that person up. Restraint in a classroom can mean letting some student ramble on; but if a teacher believes that such rambling can be used as a way to move that student into a better position to move ahead, it is a positive approach. Like most work in classrooms, it requires teachers' judgments—about some of which you and I might disagree.

Universality. This denotes the concept that something should apply to all of us, not just a special group. Most of us Americans believe that we all should enjoy the benefits of collectively designed and controlled enterprises, such as schools, public transit systems, and potable water, wherever we may find ourselves, whether in a city or in a far rural area. The exceptions among us are there, but the majority opinions still control our actions.

Safety. We desire to be safe and for our children to be safe when out of our hearing and sight. By safety, we mean both physical safety (No one will mug us) and emotional safety (I can walk my dog along the streets of our neighborhood without being sworn at), but also the safety required for the explanation of new ideas, ones that might challenge the views of those hanging on to conventional wisdom. This is important, as much of good high school teaching challenges—or should challenge—the status quo.

Linear, meaning straight, as in a straight line. Some of the time we want our students to be able to think in an orderly progression of ideas, each building on the one before. Of course, some of the time we want them to take interesting diversions away from a straight line, to explore the unexpected and imaginative. Persons who are only straight-line thinkers can be dangerous; they plunge on with their ideas and arguments even if those contentions lead us into an abyss. Persons who change their commitments at the drop of a hat are dangerous. Persisting with a worthy position (linear or otherwise) can be constructive, but hanging on to a silly idea is sure to be harmful.

Bureaucracy. A dictionary definition is "administration of a government chiefly through bureaus and departments staffed with nonelected officials." The "nonelected" characterization should be a concern; folks who are appointed are usually engaged for a term or for life until retirement age and can resist, if they have a mind to do so, the objections of others, such as schoolchildren's parents. The more we leave decisions to the bureaucracy, the less control, as a practical matter, we have. Bureaucracies can be convenient and effective, making messiness rare. However, the costs of such neatness can be great, forcing differing considerations into a single, tight mold.

Sense, as in making good sense—meaning making sense of stimuli coming from the outside. Provoking the students is what schools do, or should do. Making sense is a skill, one that requires patience. Teachers must stimulate the students, shaking them, getting their attention. Just giving students a list of things that have stimulated others misses the point. The work must make sense to each student, one by one. Sense also appears in a quite different context, such as in a sense of humor, including a sense of the absurd. Of course, the very notion of adolescence itself is in some respects absurd, an invention that marks what we have decided is a stage of life, a stage that we have invented.

Dork, meaning a stupid, inept, and foolish person. Adults do not use this word often, but many of their offspring do: "What a dork Joe is; he slows down our class and holds us back." We do not want our students to be dorks, to be inept in the classroom or outside it. Yet we also do not want our students to call one of their peers a dork, in the degrading sense, even if those students are correct in perceiving their age mate often to be silly when she makes irrelevant remarks. The whole situation can test a teacher's mettle and patience.

Etched, as in sharply etched, to make something clear and permanent. We etch the difference between adjectives and adverbs into the minds, and thus the habits, of our students. If an idea is not important enough to etch, why teach it in the first place? All serious ideas and skills deserve to be etched, meaning that they become a part of each student's intellectual equipment. The trivial can be tolerated but not expected.

Exponent, meaning one who expounds or interprets—that is, a teacher who delivers a message and then is able to bring some sense to it that makes sense to young people. The word has an important technical meaning in mathematics.

Logic, meaning an examination of the structure of a subject or idea; the skill of arranging what one knows so that young people can both make sense of it and use it. "Yes," one dutiful youngster might say, "it makes sense now; I see how adjectives give a deeper meaning to nouns."

Character, as in being a young person who acts—or acts out—in imaginative ways. Varied characters make for a lively, ever unpredictable group of adolescents. It is difficult to imagine a student who is not a character, just an animal filling space in a classroom. I have never found one in my decades of teaching.

Being prepared, as for a test, ready and even eager to tackle the questions that the teacher presents. "Being prepared" in the sense of the Scout's Motto: Be prepared for the unexpected.

• • •

The language of schooling must be clear and useful, to the extent that this is possible. Our words, consciously or unconsciously, most often signal to us and to others our actions and priorities; in this sense, our words are crucial signals to others.

At the Francis W. Parker Charter Essential School in Devens, Massachusetts, visitors are given a glossary full of the special words that are used to describe subjects, the schedule, and the progress of the students. In describing itself with these words, the community forms and clarifies itself and prepares to share itself with others. As newcomers learn these special words with their special usages—my favorite is *gateway* as a verb, to describe a student's progress through three divisions— they enjoy their unique status.

Yet our language must not be full of jargon; we cannot fall prey to that silly habit of too many educators to create and thereby to dignify some otherwise obvious point. Their mistake is that in an attempt to look deep, they turn off the very people they are trying to impress. Education jargon is the language of pedants; it identifies those who have so little confidence in themselves and their work that they seek to create a veil of words to hide them.

Until we pay close attention to the words we use, we will make little progress in the creation of the institution that every serious person will be persuaded to accept as a "*New* American High School." Most Americans, alas, pay little attention to what they say, hear, or write. They accept language as free as the air they breathe—until they travel to France, Italy, or Germany, much less to China or Korea. Visiting the latter countries is a telling experience. The difficulty of hearing and writing and decoding those languages was especially brought home to me as Nancy struggled to learn to read Chinese. Ideas displayed as characters in several Asian languages inevitably challenge the occidental mind. We were not trained in this way, but we intend to live in this world.

Some critics may find my stress on words a trivial and excessively academic exercise. "Reform doesn't arise from mere words," they will say. "Reform comes from rolling up one's sleeves and getting down to work." I believe them to be wrong. Action follows intent, and intent arises from—and becomes clearer with—language, whether audibly expressed or settled inside an actor's head. If you act before you think, you may find yourself in deep trouble. Sort out the explicit matters in your mind first—that is, speak to yourself in words that you deem appropriate, and then it will be easier to act.

Language counts. Words count. Looking carefully at a word's several possible meanings can shove unexpected new ideas into your thinking about what a *New* American High School may be like or into what it might develop. Make sure, therefore, that you have the most apt words to shape and describe the design of your school before you attend to all those important details that make up a good, new place for educating the young.

CHAPTER · SIX

Time

Clocks affect every aspect of our modern lives. Even though we accept it as a matter of course, time is a mystery. Everything in time is in motion; what we call seasons come and go so predictably that we tie our rituals around them; Christmas and Hanukkah have deep historical roots. Whether the reality (or what we accept as reality) of time is built for eternity is, for us, moot; we try to describe it, but we never created it; we accept its presence as fact.

Time, my parents told me, was precious, a commodity not to be wasted. "Stop reading those comics and get on with your homework," my mother firmly reminded me. "It is late, and you must be going to bed soon." I'd parry: "But it will only take me a minute to finish," wiggling to get out of that parental trap. "No, to bed, NOW." Some adolescents do not have such an attentive mother, but, as a kid, I didn't appreciate her orders.

Indeed, pondering about time reminds us of our imper-
manence and of the mystery of who we are, persons trying to
make sense of our aging and the rush of understanding that
it provides. *What I was last week is not what I am today. Why
did this happen? What does that difference mean? Have I wasted
my life? Have I spent time on the wrong things? What difference
will that make for me and my children? Will I be able to do all
that I want to do before I die?*

Time is the coinage of school. The clock is king. Despite
recent studies which advise us that teenagers' "biological
clocks" differ from those of younger children and adults, we
start school early when it is convenient for others but when
most adolescents are not fully awake. This causes all sorts of
problems: some we can see and some we cannot. Too many
adolescents get less sleep than they need. A yet-unwritten
paper due for delivery to an English teacher keeps the student
awake in bed that night, perhaps knowing that he must get
some rest if the essay is to be any good, yet fearful that, being
so tired, he might oversleep and never write it, or even miss
the school bus. Every student is to arrive at the appropriate
school building by, say, 8:32, and if that young laggard does
not, he will be punished.

Once in school, the ironfisted schedule guarantees chaos
in most schools between bells. As the day proceeds, everyone,
every student, every teacher with few exceptions, will change
classrooms—say, at 9:47 AM—with three minutes allotted as
"passing time." By 9:50, the hallways will be jammed with
students zigging and zagging, trying not to bump into one
another (or deliberately seeking to stumble into one another,
to get that young person's attention, to scare him or her, or

just because it is fun). Teachers can learn much from watching passing time; they can make quick judgments of who among the students are friends and who are not, who is a loner and who is not, and whether there is a troubled adolescent who needs help. It is useful information for teachers who are interested in their students, but passing time was not designed for that purpose, but for simple crowd control. The sheer numbers in most high schools greatly exacerbate the problems of time.

Nevertheless, the urgency of moving from place to place in a short amount of time works. Most youngsters find their way into their appropriate classrooms. Indeed, to the orderly mind, *place* is as important as time. Teaching starts; thirty-nine to fifty-nine minutes later, most students start eying the clock and, tuning the teacher out, start gathering their notes and textbooks together. They look forward to the break, to go to the bathroom or meet with a friend from another class or buttonhole a teacher to check on an assignment or just to be seen by that teacher. This chance to make the rounds allows the students to be known, which helps them believe that "I *am* somebody!" For them, it is a useful way to spend "their" time, to differentiate it from the school's time.

However—say, at 10:17—a bell rings, classroom doors shut, and the hallways are quiet again, save for the clatter of those late for class or the quiet talk of teachers who have a period off or who are going to a new classroom for the hour. Some sounds are coming from classrooms, creating a quiescent hum—or a dull or harsh roar which signals that not much French is being taught and learned in that language class.

Such quiescence is not the rule in many schools. Some places have never been able to inculcate the habit of "settling down," and their restless students keep at their jabbering, whatever their teacher says. Such rude inattention is exhausting for new teachers especially; they fear for their reputations. I know this from experience in my first year of teaching—my middle school kids tested me with glee—and I always wondered what my senior colleagues thought of my apparently tolerating all that talking and even laughing in my classes. They and I never brought up the subject, as it would have been too painful for all of us. However, the school in which I started my career—the Roxbury Latin School in Boston—was basically such a serious place that my students, more often than not, accommodated to its mores rather than to mine. In that school, all the students were, by virtue of the contribution that an endowment provided, scholarship enrollees, and they and their families recognized this. They worked hard, and a little levity was probably good for them. Still, if my older colleagues disapproved, these veterans probably thought that I was wasting time by tolerating any diversion from what each pupil should know.

Time also provides a form of pedagogical coinage. My subject, I might say, gets more minutes per week than yours, and therefore it *must* be more important than yours, thereby giving me stature in the academic pecking order. For example, physics, many teachers in the hard sciences and mathematics not surprisingly agree, is more important than, say, an elective social studies course that our school offers in international relations. Therefore, it ought to be allowed to add lab work to the usual number of classes. A student may believe, *Physics impresses college admissions officers and my parents.* He thinks, *Even my dad, who took physics when he was in school, is still dazzled by it all; after leafing through my textbook, he said,* "This isn't the physics I took." To most Americans, physics is a strange and impenetrable subject and is thus—irrationally perhaps—perceived as a powerful area of study. The more mysterious the discipline is, the more importance it is judged to have. Students who take physics are by that fact perceived to be attending an elite school. And many a dad (myself included) brags about "my son, the physicist."

As for other subjects, chemistry is allotted time for laboratory periods and thus receives more minutes per week than, say, a writing elective offered by the English Department or a course on economics offered by the Social Studies Department. (However, although time spent near the teacher in the science lab or the beginning language class may be necessary, time spent reading a novel as homework may make just as great a claim on a student's time.) As for the mushy, ill-described "social studies" course, unkind competitors think it is aptly named: being *social* is like a dance, such as the deliberately named Spring Social held in the gym, where the teachers have to patrol the dark corners to catch any beer drinkers or excessively amorous twosomes. If it resembles such off-hours pastimes, does social studies belong in school at all?

Artists, whether visual, musical, or theatrical, need long periods of time to accomplish the performances that are their desired outcomes, but they often have to grab that time outside the main school day. As for students of foreign languages, the best use of their time would be in shorter, smaller classes more often, but most schools cannot afford the clever scheduling officer who could somehow bring that into being. Every school's schedule is a cluster of compromises, an expression of a particular institution's academic values.

Once the daily timetable is set, time inside classrooms must be spent carefully. As with the hours assigned by the school, individual classroom minutes can be viewed as pedagogical currency. We teachers have just so many "coins," and we must "spend" them thoughtfully, on the topics that are most likely to stick in most of our students' minds—or on those that are most likely to turn up on state-mandated standardized tests. Further, we need to recognize that each student has his or her own needs for a certain amount of time; and these needs will alter as each student changes his or her mood, interests, and willingness to tackle new topics.

In my view, there is not enough time in most schools to do the job that we have accepted. Contemporary demands on high schools are substantial, and as we have added to the list of "must-covers," we have not added the minutes—the hours— that these new requirements entail. Critics say that "we can't do that," that teachers with young children at home must be able to pick them up, that other teachers must hurry off to their second jobs. The critics also argue about the financial costs involved, saying that "the public will not stand for additional expense." Americans, of course, are used to rising costs in many public enterprises, such as the U.S. Postal Service. Few pause to ponder the need for rational priorities in the design of a strong secondary school, or the money that such planning will require.

Some educators argue that taking the time to push adolescents to learn how to be informed, civilized, and conscientious young adults is perhaps the most important argument for compulsory schooling, far more important, say, than the details involved in fathoming the meaning and uses of Ohm's Law. Rather, these educators might say, the students must learn how to get along and even protect a society that values personal freedom and an ethic of hard, principled work, whether that work is in the kitchen or at a law office, in a large grocery store, as part of a carpenters' team, or as a lonely poet. Again, not all students master these matters in the same number of hours, any more than all patients recovering from surgery heal at a rigidly predictable rate.

And then there are sports. *In sana, corporae sano*, the ancients observed; a sound mind deserves a sound body, and recent studies have reaffirmed that moderate exercise improves one's ability to learn. The recent obsession with testing, however, has caused a cutback in the time allotted to exercise, or even recess, which is going to be harmful unless we find a way to have both serious academics and adequate exercise.

Although being on a team is rarely a requirement, in many schools athletics get the most minutes of the school day that a high school offers, especially during the afternoon, with mandatory weekend games and drills. Sport, some critics will say, swamp everything else in the school program. The nonfiction account by H. G. Bissinger, *Friday Night Lights: A Town, a Team, and a Dream*, about a high school in Odessa, Texas, and how its football team dominated the academic calendar, painfully describes a case in point. That Friday evening game provided a fine—and usually badly needed—meeting place for adult citizens along with their offspring, these across ethnic groups and races, where they could come together, becoming a useful melting pot of clear significance. In that town, football players were chosen in a hierarchical fashion—the older, more skilled, and bigger getting the choice positions—but the fans at their games assembled both freely and equitably. There surely was civic virtue in all those bright Friday lights, but Bissinger also shows the ways that football's dominance weakened necessary academic pursuits and, thus, the institution as a whole.

I have long respected this device of using time as the coinage of schooling, and I lived by it while I was a high school principal. At the large private boarding school where I served as headmaster—Phillips Academy at Andover—some courses got more minutes than did others, importance defined solely by what tradition and college admissions requirements dictated.

English, mathematics, science (again, physics, for example), history (sometimes including the social sciences), and art (visual and performance) were the staples of the program. A carefully designed bit of "independent study" in an academic field would "count." Learning how to play the cello would not "count," but playing the cello in the school orchestra would. An off-campus job serving as an assistant to a veterinarian would not "count," nor would tutoring younger students. Although most adults would agree that much useful material might be learned in such enterprises, their worth would be too personal, too hard to measure. Thus these areas of study were presumably less worthy than their more "rigorous" cousins to earn the carefully guarded and distributed academic credit, and time spent on them would have to yield its own reward.

While I was at Andover in the late 1970s, Mortimer J. Adler, the controversial University of Chicago philosopher, invited me to join what he called the Paideia Group (of which I was, sad to say, the only participant who was fully engaged in a career in secondary education). Mortimer was a wonderfully stubborn and likeable man. Much of our discussion centered around the best possible use of the time available in the high school years. We group members peppered Mortimer with objections to his view of the pedagogical world—he loved that word *pedagogy*; he politely listened to us and then, with great charm, wrote up what he personally believed, this expressed in a simple one-page chart comprising three columns: Acquisition of Organized Knowledge; Development of Intellectual Skills—Skills of Learning; and Enlarged Understanding of Ideas and Values, this "by means of Maieutic or Socratic Questioning and Active Discussion." He outlined each of the columns' "operations and activities." Clearly many of these activities were to involve active engagement by the students in their own learning. No passive receptacles here!

My point here is not to disinter, praise, or criticize the Paideia manifesto but, rather, to note the limited attention given to *time* in the report. Special arrangements were to be made both for the strugglers and the academic high fliers, but scant attention was paid to other reasons besides natural talent that might affect the pace of learning. There was no mention of the rapidly climbing influence of the media on the development of children. The lives of his hypothetical students were disentangled from the families each had and the communities in which each lived, as though who your parents and siblings were or where you lived were of limited importance.

These omissions were more obvious to the individuals involved with schools than to the others gathered around Adler's table. Outnumbered as I was, I never succeeded in convincing him to include them in his deliberations. However, I suspect that in the Paideia schools that have been founded since the manifesto, such considerations have earned respect and have affected the way schedules are put together. In spite of the controversial aspects of Adler's work, his insistence that schools ought aggressively to promote the careful use of one's mind, and his feisty, blunt assessments should today be taken seriously in the design or redesign of a secondary school. In that context, *The Paideia Proposal* should today reappear on the reading lists of courses in schools of education. (In Nancy's and my course in the Harvard Graduate School of Education thirty years later, we almost apologetically introduced it as "perhaps a little dated," but our students were fascinated, more with the ideas than with the controversy.)

• • •

All that said, how would a high school function if its authorities took *time* seriously?

It would have more time for teaching and learning, more than the 180 days per year and more than the six hours per day that obtain in most jurisdictions.

It would operate on a twelve-month basis, with students and staff rotating in and out, allowing some "vacation" for rest and the recharging of intellectual batteries, a pattern that conforms with most of the working world.

It would function on a schedule that had blocks of time of differing lengths, thus providing opportunities for the variation of time necessary, given the nature of the subject, the extent to which it was to be taught, the experience of the staff, the qualification of students, and the depth of a school's library and laboratories. Teachers could match what they wanted to teach over a period of school days, given the time lengths available.

It would arrange for new teachers to start with a reduced load in order to allow them to spend more time planning classes, designing assessments, and observing and speaking with colleagues.

It would have the flexibility to listen to its teachers and allow them to do some horse-trading, subject to the principal's approval.

"I'll give you my early-morning ninety-minute block if you'll give me some shorter bits of time that I could use flexibly. I have kids this term who squirm incessantly! I can keep them 'on task,' but only in smaller and more frequent periods."

"I'm new to this subject, and I badly need extra time to plan and then to teach it. I may not get it just right the first time, and I may need to circle around and take more time with it."

"My kids in B block are at all sorts of levels. I need to have flexible time to cope with this. Some of the youngsters will 'get' what they missed quickly. Others will take my repeating it over and over again."

"We had two snow days last month, and my classes are way behind. I need more time to catch up. The seniors must be ready for their SATs and state tests by April."

"I'm going on maternity leave, and I don't know for exactly how long or how much my baby may need me after birth. It will certainly change me in how I view other people's children, and it will inevitably alter the ways that I teach. Give me time to sort all this out—and give time to my colleagues to plan just how they might help 'return' me to the school."

(You will notice that in none of these requests to juggle time is there a request for *less* time—which is why I suggest a longer school year.)

In this last example, of course, there are many issues besides time being juggled here. A new member of a family changes everything. The miracle is that so many families handle it gracefully. Alas, in our time, few grandparents, as a practical matter, are able to help out at their children's houses. Families scatter. If your grandchildren live in Tucson, Arizona, and you live in Bangor, Maine, regular, sustained contact between the generations is practically impossible. And there is always a chance that the baby's parents will separate, leaving the little ones primarily with one of the adults. The joys and sorrows of family life—not just for its students but for its teachers—have a tremendous influence on the work of a school.

A thoughtful school designer must pay attention to all these matters and find a sensible accommodation for each request, which will be more likely if there is more time.

• • •

Time remains something over which, save in unexpected emergencies, we can have limited control. Recall the tale of the tortoise and the hare. The latter sneers at the former as being insufferably slow to walk, and leaps off to make his point. In time, the hare wearies and lays down to take a nap. Soon the tortoise comes upon him and keeps going, arriving at the finish line first. The message to students: *Never give up; take your own time, but persist. You will get there whether you are a hare or a tortoise.*

There are obvious messages here for teachers and principals—and district and state authorities who all too often decide to microdesign as though each school were exactly the same as every other:

- Keep the schedule simple, thereby allowing its application to be complex.

- Let each student proceed at the rate that represents his or her best effort. Do not praise the "quick" and humiliate the "slow." Use the time in the classroom to let each succeed or come as close to success as is possible.

- Keep the daily schedule loose, thereby allowing alterations as conditions unexpectedly change.

- Spend faculty meetings as occasions where adjustments can be made, these on the basis of recent events, such as a major snowstorm or a rash of illness among the students and staff.

- Let the shape of the subject being taught define the likely time available.

- Be flexible: one class of students may need more time to get its minds around a particular subject than another. Even within the classroom, there will be those who need less, or more, time, with a further effect on the homework that he or she can do.

- Be patient—and imaginative. If a lesson seems to miss with some of the students, teach it in a different way.

- Arrange the calendar for a four-"period" day, each "class period" being ninety minutes. Concentrate on a core program of English, mathematics, science, arts, and a foreign language (the choice here varying as a school is situated—for example, French in Maine and Spanish in Texas).

- Keep decisions close to the action—for example, let a pair of teachers (say, one in art and one in mathematics) devise the use of the time allotted to them and arrange who the particular children will be in these sections.

- Allow wide discretion by individual teachers as to how those minutes are used. Expect the principal or assistant principals to drop in and out of classrooms to assist where needed and to make adjustments as required.

Such sensible practices will upset the commonly rigid schedule set for a school, those fixed allotments of time that serve the purposes of governing boards, state inspectors, bigshot visitors, textbook publishers (a set curriculum allows for big press runs of large books), and the school's administration (which may enjoy a predictable and easily supervised daily program). They will reward instead the reasonable needs of the students in general and liven up the program. Teachers with special expertise will be able to help each other and mix up the routines when desirable. Flexibility will allow a subset of students to take a trip to hear a candidate for public office speak and answer questions. If these opportunities are provided at different times to different students, fundamental fairness, if not strict equality, will be offered.

I agree that all this will play hob with the planning of the year's work. A close example of such a flexible routine is a well-designed hospital's emergency department, a place where no one knows exactly what will appear until the ambulances arrive. Another example is the painter's studio. The artist may have a quite detailed plan in mind (in her mind's eye, so to speak) when she first puts charcoal to canvas. Yet another is the progress of, say, a football game. The team has a book of plays with which every player is familiar but that must be adapted to fit what is happening on the field.

Good schools should resemble these dynamic kinds of workplaces rather than the ordered places that they try—futilely—to be. Indeed, life itself—and especially life with teenagers and with those who have chosen to spend time with them—is full of surprises. There may be a strong wind, making outside work difficult on the one day you have available. It rains. Or it does not rain. The time-absorbing class clown comes to school. Or he does not come to school. Maybe he even moves away. (Hallelujah? No comment.)

Learning is messy, and always has been. Each child's progress or lack of progress is usually unpredictable. One gets sick. Another has a crisis at home. A third by some mysterious happening "gets" what he earlier failed to understand. Key decisions must be made by the person or persons closest to the action, but always keeping in mind that, as my mother told me, time must not be wasted, at least in school, though even there it is sometimes hard to distinguish what is worthwhile and what is not.

So be it. Change is inexorable, however disconcerting both those aspects may be. Teachers and students will be more likely to accept change if they feel that they understand it and will be the ones managing it. The best use of time will vary according to contexts, and we must be alert to all their nuances. Successful educators accept these challenges and then embrace them.

CHAPTER · SEVEN

Space and Costs

Where one learns and teaches makes a difference. Space affects how you feel and think. What one gives up to accomplish a task—dreaming up a new sort of school, for example—implies a cost, often a substantial cost in money, time, energy, and imagination. Yet it must be done, for mindlessly following an outdated plan is costly as well.

I have experienced the space issue at every place where I have worked. At Boston's Roxbury Latin School during the 1950s, the building in which I taught had been deliberately and threateningly designed. The seventh-grade classroom seated forty-four boys; I taught these youngsters in two groups of twenty-two, and there were but a few absentees; these were on the whole working- and middle-class children, often Jewish and Roman Catholics, and missing school or turning a paper in late to a teacher was sinful.

I also taught eighth graders, and immediately noticed that their room was a bit smaller than the space they had experienced as seventh graders. The assumption was clear that a predictable number of the latter had flunked out or had been withdrawn by their parents when the signals grew ominous: gaining admission to another school was considered a more dignified step than being pitched out by Roxbury Latin authorities. Again, the ninth-grade room also was reduced in size. By the time the students hit the twelfth grade, they enjoyed a small, cozy seminar-type room, with shelves of reference books on the wall. The silent message to students and parents was eloquent: only the successful scholars will survive. This led to my students' being hardworking—but some were quite fearful.

Australia's Melbourne Grammar School, where I next taught, had a mix of buildings, most of which reflected different eras and priorities than ours. The majority were built of magnificent blue stone (an Australian staple), and the campus, usually shimmering with moist, flowering bushes, was beautiful. However, the inside of my classroom was always damp, cramped, and, during the summer (our North American winter), hot. We had a fan to ease the sweating and to circulate some air: the punka, a device borrowed from India, a single oblong board suspended from the ceiling with a rope attached to it. The students, one boy at a time, were assigned to stand and pull that rope. It may not have furthered his education much, but it helped the rest of us. I especially benefited from it, as I was expected (as were all of the instructors) to teach in an open-front black academic gown, a raiment that gave dignity, if not comfort, to my semitheistic profession.

When we moved from Australia back to Cambridge, we rented apartments, but when I had earned my PhD, Nancy and I bought an attached but serviceable house that had a separate apartment on the third floor. We believed that we could rent this space out to a student who was interested in doing some child care for us to lower the rental cost: x hours of sitting = y hours of reduced rent. This worked well for us except that we got quickly to know these young people and enjoyed their company, thus reducing the number of hours we went out. Instead, we looked forward to staying home, playing pick-up soccer with our tiny kids, our tenants, and visiting nephews and nieces in the front hall, with the sliding doors to living and dining rooms pulled to allow the appropriate width of the "goal" (the younger the goalie, the narrower the goal). In that space, youth defeated age again and again.

During the Cambridge years, we also bought twenty-four acres of forest property in the small town of Harvard to the west of Cambridge with some money that Nancy's father left us in his will. That wonderful man would have liked that we invested in property; he was a great woods walker. After a couple of years, when it was clear that I would stay at Harvard Graduate School of Education (HGSE) as its dean, we built a small home—the architect called it a "camp"—on some of that land, for use as a weekend and summer home. Although the Black Panthers phoned us there during the student turmoil in 1969 and caused me to drive quickly back to Cambridge for an afternoon of dealing with "nonnegotiable demands," on the whole we credit having our relatively stable and happy family life to that retreat. That setting, with its long dirt driveway and its spectacular view to the west, remains our full-time home to this day. Children and dogs love to visit. So do eagles, crows, woodchucks, and deer. We gaze at Mount Wachusett during most Sunday mornings while we listen to the services at Harvard University's Memorial Church on the radio. We have the smug feeling that most of that church's congregation (and choir) would envy us our coffee and big sky as we listen and pray, but perhaps they prefer to be just where they are.

As I became an administrator at Harvard, my relationship with space changed. I no longer was just handed an office and told to cope with it; I had to keep up the old space and provide for the new, so that others could get on with *their* work. HGSE was growing; we moved from the cramped Lawrence Hall (which no longer exists, replaced by a new science center) to a former Radcliffe building, Longfellow Hall, on Appian Way. We also built Larsen Hall, which was opened just after I became dean, for faculty offices, seminar rooms, and a large lecture hall; and, a few years later, I had the responsibility to raise money and build the Gutman Library to contain all the university's considerable holdings in education. Thus we were given the usually rare opportunity to shape these buildings to meet our particular needs.

Phillips Academy—where we moved after more than a decade studying, teaching, and "deaning" at Harvard—has many nineteenth- and even a few eighteenth-century buildings, and although few were air-conditioned, all could easily catch some breezes. I had no trouble coping with climate there, and suffered only in bitter cold and snowy weather, when the heat from the school's power plant could not keep up with falling temperatures. We also had some anxious moments when the kind of oil we required was temporarily withheld by the OPEC cartel during the mid-1970s. The best place to be on a cold, damp day was always at the gym by the pool, enjoying its steamy, moist climate.

Many of the grand old buildings, most made of wood, had been labeled as national landmarks, and the school, as well as others who owned such buildings, could not compromise the exteriors. We paid for their upkeep—which cost a pretty penny—and we could move around what was indoors, so long as we did not alter the basic design of the footings, posts, and beams. We also renovated the dining hall, the gym, and a few other areas to accommodate the girls who were attending the school for the first time.

After I left Andover to return to the town of Harvard and direct the Study of High Schools, we rented a tiny office in Cambridge, but most of us did most of our work on the road or writing in our own homes. Slowly, the computer enabled me to write on my own rather than be tied to an assistant.

When I went to lead the Education Department at Brown, my offices were larger and more capable of entertaining visitors—mostly my students. I also held several of my smaller classes in the evening at our home, which was about a half-hour's walk from campus. When, in retirement, we returned again to Harvard, we quickly became involved with local friends in the launch of the Francis W. Parker Charter Essential School sited on an old Army base, Fort Devens. After several years, including the year in which Nancy and I were "acting co-principals" in a windowless building, we inherited (and eventually purchased) the Army's former elementary school and added to it a few years later by buying serviceable units from a nearby district that had used them while the major renovation of their permanent high school was under way. You might call this transaction somewhat of a "marriage of convenience," but it served its occupants well. Better yet, we could afford it without endangering our favorable teacher-student ratio.

• • •

This is the point for those who are designing a New American High School: all space anywhere carries costs. If weather conditions require central heating and air conditioning, the costs of oil and unending upkeep are substantial. One cannot plan a new school without carefully analyzing and planning with these not-so-humble matters in mind. Centuries ago, our predecessor teachers understood this, and their monasteries, though usually damp, were habitable because all had to dress warmly. It is no surprise in our day to find the traditional garb of university graduates, priests, bishops, cardinals, and even the pope to be gorgeously resplendent—and able to handle the draftiest, foulest weather. Geography shapes what must be done, to an unavoidable degree; colder latitudes require more protection than those in the south, but southerners are more likely to have to cope with sweaty summer days, insects, and rot.

Planners of new schools have to consider space and cost issues carefully from the very beginning. They must study a large-scale map in order to select the site for the new school with an eye toward the convenience of those who will use it; the shorter student and faculty traveling time required each day, the better the likely attendance. Does the site of the school influence what the demographics of the school will be? Do you have to be in a high-rent area to get middle-class kids (and middle-class parents)?

Each decision must be weighed with costs in mind, and not just costs in terms of money, but also in time, and—these days—in the use of energy. Can students and teachers walk safely to school? What will it cost to hire safety monitors to shepherd youngsters across busy streets and, in the winter, icy sidewalks? Who will those monitors be? Teachers picking up some extra cash for this extra work? Administrators doing one of their traditional jobs? Parents volunteering their time? Older kids?

What sites are nearest to public transportation? What are the possibilities for parking that is dedicated and policed for school use? If you will need your own buses, how many vehicles will you need, and what will each cost? There are substantial and continuing expenses here.

In the most recent decade, when Nancy and I were teaching a seminar in school design, the placement of the school in nature was important to a number of our students. Designing outdoor space in which students could play or garden was part of their plans, important adjuncts to the students' program. When told to design schools in metropolitan areas, some even attempted to create an oasis outside the building as well as within. Both cost and the use of the students' time—scarce commodities—had to be considered in these calculations, but our graduate school designers offered a vigorous defense for their decisions and—mostly—won over their critics.

As your planning of a truly *new* American high school proceeds, do some "gaming," pitting the possible sites against each
other. "If we site the school here, what will our 'entrance' and
'exit' costs in time and money be? What time will school start?"
Staggering the starting times (seniors arriving at 8:00 AM,
juniors at 8:20 AM, and so forth) will ease inevitable conges-
tion—but this requires a stable age-specific school population,
an assumption that is efficient only when carried out by others
who may then need to be hired for other jobs during the day.
Do a cost-benefit analysis, contrasting the several options.
Bounce these off of experienced outsiders. Ponder all this and
do not move on until the majority of you are confident that you
have chosen the best alternative.

All these issues raise important policy questions. In years
of teaching at Brown and Harvard, when I offered my students
the chance to design their own high schools, most of their
plans assumed that the way we teach is still the way that we
have always taught. When I was involved in designing the
Parker School in the 1990s, I too was drawn to the more
familiar pattern. Yet planners might sensibly start with different premises. For example:

First, challenge the notion that we collectively—through
the state—have the obligation to educate all our children
by means of formal, school-building-based collective schooling. Might there be effective alternatives, such as a mix of
homeschooling and in-school schooling? Or computer-based
lessons that can engage students anywhere? Or in space shared
with other enterprises, such as a community college or public
library?

Second, brainstorm some alternatives to today's typical school that is a building open to all at once and empty most of the rest of the time. A friend who started a school in an urban area was dismayed by how many of her students had a problem with obesity. One solution was to situate her buildings at considerable distances from one another; in this way, she tackled two issues at once. In another cost-cutting, flexible example, you can operate on a four-season basis, with students enrolling for three, or perhaps in special circumstances, two semesters.

Third, examine each of the state's educational and assessment goals and decide which are, in your view, legitimate state functions; which can be shaved a bit here and there; and which, in your judgment, are no business of the state, such as matters of moral and religious education. Caring for your children with "special needs" should be a state responsibility, with the expenses for any one child spread across the citizens as a whole. However, the laws in many states don't allow for such common sense, causing difficult problems for both families and small schools.

Fourth, survey the public resources available to higher education, to public libraries, and to public radio and public television; ascertain which of these could be argued to be applicable to the elementary and secondary grades as well. Although these institutions are not likely to want to share their money, they may be delighted to share their products with the children in a local school.

Fifth, assemble a variety of plans for your school or school system. In that process, persistently question the appropriateness—the logical implications—of the term *system* for what you desire. The word implies the need for an orderly plan. Remind the higher-ups, including political leaders, that the best of human intellectual activity is not, in fact, orderly and that some human needs and abilities can be crippled by too much uniform channeling. The metaphor of the soaring mind is better. Each younger or older mind tests the limits of what it sees and has been left to ponder. *What*, that mind says, *can I imagine that doesn't fit the conventional understandings? What mysteries are there to pierce?* How can one cajole every student into letting her or his mind soar? Must every attempt to do so be a costly one?

• • •

Some people complain that schools cost too much, no matter what goes on inside them. Challenge the attitudes of citizens who argue that these prosaic matters of space are easily settled by the question, "What is cheapest?" Convince them that once human imagination and connection enter the picture, there is much more to the matter of housing than mere bricks and mortar.

Place counts. What you do in each place counts even more as you gather your people and establish the setting for serious learning.

CHAPTER · EIGHT

Courses

Students in high schools take "courses," but mostly they are dominated—and limited—by subjects.

Subject is a forceful word, one with many meanings that we must ponder. "You are *subject* to my authority." That is, you are at my beck and call. "You are a *subject* within my control. I rule you." Another meaning, not directly related to the first one, is an area of study to be distinguished from others. One might say, "Math is her best *subject*," but also "You must learn this *subject*." The concept of a separate subject was an invention, not a discovery—mathematics was not found under a rock—but in many minds there has come to be an almost biblical belief that certain subjects are central to a good education.

My introduction to subjects started in kindergarten. "Now we will do our letters: A, B, C." We were given cardboard posters with names of subjects on them. Cat. Dog. Mother. Car. Our teacher, Miss

Gillette, made a game of these poster boards. She would hold one up for all of us to see: "What does this say?" she would ask us. Sometimes there was silence, other times a chorus of correct responses or answers that were far off base. She would go through a number of cards and then repeat them, in a new order. If we all correctly identified one of them, she would put it aside and continue with the rest. Somehow she arranged it that all of our pile of cards would be identified by all of her students before the end of the day. We were all to be winners, and winners often remember fondly the occasions of their triumph.

The target was that, eventually, somehow or other, all of us would be legitimate winners. *Legitimacy* was not a word that we little ones knew, but we did know pretty well what the "right" answers were. We also knew—most of the time—whether we really knew those right answers or whether we just listened to our neighbors. Our goal was the same as that of our teachers: to outgrow the need to pretend and to know how to read for ourselves. Our teachers indicated that "catching on to reading" would happen naturally over time. Because it was a somewhat progressive school, there was less competition over how much time it would take.

In recent times, this classroom process has been designed on the basis of what we know about early learning. Time is important and must not be wasted. There is now more method and intervention in the teaching of reading; more is known about the sequence of experiences most likely to serve each student of whatever chronological age well. There is also more womanpower available, and the slower readers may be taken aside by an aide to review the words that the teacher has chosen. Perhaps the student is embarrassed by his need for help, but perhaps he is also grateful when he realizes that he is no longer waiting for his neighbor but instead is reading on his own. The subject is reading; the subject is also the number of interesting topics and stories that become available to the child as her skill increases, at school but also at home.

Teaching in the Army gave me these new perspectives on the nature of subjects, but there are, of course, many other experiences that help teachers relate the process of investigating topics to acquiring useful learning. In my own career, after two years in the classroom and a master of arts in teaching degree, I settled into working on my PhD. There my scholarship revolved around the concept of subjects.

I was interested in the rapid growth of public high schools at the end of the nineteenth century, a time when the curriculum was in flux, and, then as now, new schools were eager for guidance. I was lucky enough to delve into the report of the so-called Committee of Ten on Secondary School Studies, chaired by Harvard University's supremely self-confident president, Charles William Eliot. There were, he preached, five universal subjects: mathematics, science, English, foreign languages, and art (by which Eliot meant primarily visual art). To this day, more than one hundred years later, these "main line" disciplines continue without any challenge. Schools are organized into departments around their names. They are the core of much of the national and state testing that dominates education policy and practice to this day.

Behind these so-called core and required subjects is a history. In the late nineteenth century, many influential university educators and state school authorities were increasingly concerned about the readily documented "chaos" (as they put it) in what we have come to call middle and high schools. As a matter of course many decades ago, in many schools the students enrolled and left when they felt like it or when their duties on their families' farms demanded their labor. That is, the time they spent in school, when push came to shove, was secondary to their engagement with efforts that appeared to get them further along in life.

These excessively flexible schools were termed "Academies" and were the educational staples of rural and small-town America at the time. They came and went on the basis of fee-paying students or persons who appeared ready and willing to teach. Many of these Academy instructors were male preachers-in-the-making; they taught as way of supporting themselves while they prepared for entry into their religious duties. Once they gained appointment as ministers, they left their schools. By the late nineteenth century, this condition was increasingly seen as an American embarrassment, a condition that would cause European nations to scoff, yet once again, that "those standardless Yankees are rubes . . . ," or words to that effect.

This situation caught the attention of Eliot, one the most respected figures in American higher education. He may not have cared what the Europeans said, but he wanted young men to come to Harvard College ready to learn what their professors wanted to teach. That required more uniformity, and uniformity led to subjects. With some help from his assistants, he gathered information and applied his judgment to assign what he identified as "main line" subjects and others as more peripheral. Once settled on his message, Eliot sought the collaboration of the national commissioner of education, William Torrey Harris, then also the superintendent of the St. Louis Public Schools. The appointment of a superintendent of a midwestern public school system was designed to give the impression that the panel was representative of the whole nation. Few knew that he had attended Phillips Academy at Andover and Yale College. Furthermore, Harris had other qualifications as well. He was seriously interested in modern philosophy and public education. He launched a scholarly publication—the *Journal of Speculative Philosophy*—which gave him national stature. Here was a man who could stand up to Harvard's president, and, to his credit, Eliot valued that quality.

Eliot and Harris persuaded eight more prominent college and school leaders to join them, and they obtained some financial support from the financier Andrew Carnegie, who shared their concern about public education. "The Ten," as they were called, met several times, in different settings from Massachusetts to Missouri. Their powerfully influential report, sponsored by the National Educational Association (now called the National Education Association), had enormous effect, thanks to Harris's efforts through the emerging national teaching profession; the report provided guidance to the communities across the country that were building their high schools and that needed a curricular road map designed by a national authority (not some local yokel) in order to sell their plans to the often-skeptical communities that were being asked to tax themselves to make a high school possible.

Many aspects of the committee interested me, especially Eliot's justification for the subjects he promoted. He used the term "mental muscles" instinctively, especially when referring to mathematics, but without reference to research in biology that is available today. What he seemed to be saying was that most future American students would need minds that were more skilled and broadly informed in order to pursue a wide range of occupations. In that, he was surely right.

Some sixty years later, another Harvard president, James Bryant Conant, conducted a national study of the high schools and issued a concise but extensive report (*The American High School Today* [New York: McGraw-Hill, 1959]) on secondary education that also emphasized the traditional subjects. He called for

> individualized programs, required programs for all which included four years of English, three or four years of social studies, including two years of history (one of which should be American history) and a senior course in American problems or American government . . . one year of mathematics in the ninth grade (algebra or general mathematics), and at least one year of science in the ninth or tenth grade, which might well be biology or general physical science. . . . This academic program of general education involved nine or ten courses with homework to be taken in four years and occupy more than half of the time of most students, whatever their elective programs. . . . [T]he students should be grouped according to ability, subject by subject. (pp. 45–47, 49)

Conant went on to express "very special concern for the very slow learners," recommending "ability grouping" and other ways to address the problems of those "with special needs" (pp. 49, 55). He insisted that half of the English program be devoted to "Composition" and that "no English teacher should be responsible for more than one hundred pupils" (pp. 50–51).

Unlike Eliot, Conant hit the road, explaining and urging adoption of his plan at high schools across the country. The report had an immense impact; a principal who called his or her school a "Conant" school would thereby receive admiration and, more important, political protection from all those who were suspicious of change, especially the ones on the local school board. Conant recommended that small high schools be merged so that a broader curriculum could be offered. American high schools as Conant defined and designed them are now so typical that there is little interest in exploring his arguments and concerns about the curriculum he outlined. High school is what Conant said it should be. Alas, most American educators today have never heard of Conant. More's the pity; they know little about where so many of their habits came from.

Both Eliot and Conant described the entire intellectual universe as if every thought or fact could be put in one box or another. Over the century, the subjects grew into disciplines, and respected psychologists like Howard Gardner described the distinctive ways in which historians or poets or physicists think. Still, for all these interesting differences, less attention was paid to the similarities in their thinking or to the connections between them that might make their thinking richer and more productive. Again, it does not have to be this way; the so-called disciplines or subjects are convenient arrangements—inventions, not discoveries.

The challenges of our day are similar in that the supply of information still seems chaotic, but they are different in that so many students want to be engaged as well as merely informed. Most subjects envisioned by Eliot and Conant were taught separately. However, how can one proceed in physics without mastering the mathematics on which that subject depends, even if that mathematics is not exactly what the teachers or the testers desire? Much of physics is understandable and useful only when that discipline is addressed visually. Little good comes without the student's ability to see and sketch—to "use" the visual arts—both in mathematics and in three-dimensional models which that student might need in order to illumine some small piece of a topic.

In like manner, some of the techniques of social science depend on mathematics. What political polls might appear to tell you requires an astute grasp of the science of statistics; indeed, candidates for public office have been known (alas) to stress some part of a poll for political gain. Immediately after the polls close, we are subjected to assured comments by each candidate's handlers that "this proves that we are really ahead" or that "my opponent will surely twist the figures to embellish his weak credentials, exhibiting once again his or her habit of saying or doing anything to win." Both those charges may prove far from accurate when a skeptic takes the time to study the data.

The ordering of subjects is one way to make sense of a confusing world. It emerges almost unbidden from each of our minds and routines. One of us may have a particular routine in how we navigate the supermarket; weaving our way through the aisles helps us individualize our journey, make it more productive and meaningful.

However, schools aren't supermarkets: as Arthur Powell, Eleanor Farrar, and David Cohen put it, shopping mall high schools may encourage teenagers to express personal preferences, but they don't necessarily fulfill the important public mission of a well-educated adult and citizen. So we need to reorder Eliot's subjects, break up the more hidebound aspects of their monopoly, and at the same time respect the breadth implied in their vision.

There are a number of ways that we might invent new subjects for the curriculum. Is there an important new, coherent area of study and research that can be usefully teased out of the rapidly emerging media, one more incisive than the passive media studies? Is there a conjunction of art, theoretical science, language, technology, and mathematics that might be fashioned? Or will the basic thinking behind each subject reorder itself from within rather than by taking a new name— as seems to be happening, these days, to the subject of English as it incorporates semiotics into its usual fare of literature? What about geography, the study of the earth and its features and of the distribution of life on earth, including human life and the effects of human activity?

Is "sense making" a discipline that can be usefully crafted into a subject? Is human intelligence, including emotional intelligence (as Daniel Goleman defines it)? Is there the making of a subject lurking behind Howard Gardner's theory of multiple intelligences?

Knowledge and the context in which it is used are in constant flux. We may make that clearer to our students by tying our knowledge, both gained and sought after, to questions of interest to them—what we in the Coalition of Essential Schools call "essential questions." There is a task worth doing here, one that might surely make Charles William Eliot proud. He was an intellectual risk taker, and he would want us to be inventors too.

• • •

When we are casting about for a new way to consider subjects, we might think about courses. *Courses* imply journeys, movement, not necessarily defined by boundaries. Let's take a longer look at the meaning of the word.

A *course* is an "onward movement in a particular direction," the *Random House Dictionary* tells us. It means "progress," such as in "the course of events." Or a "course of water." *Course* denotes a "route . . . or path . . . a mode of action or behavior." A course is a complete body of prescribed skills constituting a curriculum. Rivers have courses. We use the word in conversation, such as "Of course you can drive me to the grocery store on this snowy day."

Course is a nice, useful, and clean word to describe a plan for study, an arrangement of ideas, knowledge, and skills that make sequential sense. It implies continuity and an organized sequence of topics and increasingly demanding intellectual skills, all this presented over a designated period of time. Given their simplicity and convenience, courses are used by state and local educational authorities to lay out what each school will offer and what each of that school's students should be able to complete.

Given their convenience, courses are a rational tool for policymakers: pieces on a checkerboard. It makes school design and governance a matter of moving those pieces from space to space. A school can have "double courses" (for, say, a science lab) or "half courses," such as one of the arts that connects with another subject, say English, where the students may be asked to prepare a visual representation of one of their own emotions. Most senior high schools require sixteen courses as the minimum for a diploma.

Many students may not know very much at all about what they may be learning. As their school day is increasingly divided into separate courses, they may struggle to see them as coherently as one can see a meal. Trying to figure out what the ideas and facts just presented to them might mean for them in their lives, they struggle to imagine a future emerging from their current concerns. Our courses may be carefully laid out, connected to a textbook and to state standards, but the students' attention will wander. The teacher's voice, however loud, may appear as a set of nonsense syllables in the young person's mind; the words in the textbook may blur together; the youngster may while away the time filling in capital O's with smiley faces.

The problem is that our curricula are not nicely detailed menus for consumption. Offerings do not proceed in a rational way. Students do not devour—all at the same pace and thus at the same time—the content and skills that we wish them to learn; here again we face the curse of regimentation, which reflects the assumption that every young person learns what we wish him or her to learn at the same time as every other youngster of the same age group, as if they were on an assembly line.

The course-counting practice is convenient and tidy ("You need to succeed at four courses each of the twelve semesters to earn a diploma") but misleading. It assumes that the algebra learned in the ninth grade is still remembered well enough to help in solving chemistry problems two years later. It expects that every adviser will know each of his or her students well enough to gauge accurately what that young person should do and, as a result, move that student steadily and carefully through his or her requirements for graduation.

It further assumes that knowledge stands still, that fresh research and experience (such as the catastrophe of the Iraq War) need not be accommodated, at least not yet. Some students may push against this rigidity ("My dad just came home from Iraq, and he says that what we read in the newspapers is misleading"). For many teachers, such remarks by their students are threatening. Connections with the present issues that may be on the students' minds lead to unwelcome confusion. How to cope not only with the fresh subject matter but also with the emotion behind it?

All that said, there *are* skills and habits that most American parents and politicians today devoutly wish that every one of our students would learn, these being the necessary minima for successful functioning in a thriving democracy. Despite their importance, very few of these are specifically taught in courses—but they could be.

- The skill of listening, and making some sense of what is heard. "Read my lips." "The check is in the mail." "I love you."

- The skill of expressing, using just the right words that describe what you have in mind. Terrible mistakes have happened in the past when what was said was not heard—or at least understood and taken seriously—as the speaker was sloppy in his or her expression and in the body language that accompanied it.

- The skill of empathy, sensing and evaluating what appears to be displayed.

- The habit of restraint, of holding back when one is unsure or when there is tension in the room.

- The habit of responsible autonomy—taking care of oneself, picking up the messes one has made. Being ready and at the right street corner to be picked up by the school bus. Walking or riding one's bike rather than expecting a parent to drive you to a friend's house.

- The habit of attending to the legitimate needs of others, friends and family members, including animals. Babysitting your younger sibling, including giving him a bottle and changing his diapers.

- The habit of wonderment, the practice of the creatively wandering mind. Such minds have produced most of our culture's new knowledge. *What if I looked at this matter in a new way?* a scholar of any age might ask. The habit of creative and informed wonderment should be an objective of any course. But how to set up such a project with different students? And how to assess how much they were helped by it?

These crucial attributes are not usually taught methodically because they don't lend themselves to a classroom structure. Half the students may already be empathic, and the other half may not be ready even to understand it. Some may learn such a habit from reading a good novel; others may require a moral discussion or even a catastrophe from which he can learn after the fact. Time and attention must be paid, but on a case-by-case basis.

Given all this, what are the considerations that educators must give to the momentous issue of what is taught in high school? What courses should be required in the school programs of all young citizens? Should those courses be defined on the basis of subjects, of the shape of a scholarly field, say, physics? Or should they arise from some aspect of thinking, and thereby knowledge? If not the traditional main lines, what then? What might replace, or supplement, them? There are a variety of ways to address these matters. Let me describe two that make my point and might be useful:

1. Expression and the Arts

The processes of communication by means of language or skillful behavior: speaking, gesturing, writing, painting, printing

Classes might include writing short essays describing, say, the meaning for each pupil of Christmas or Hanukkah. Debates could be held on historically or geographically far-off political topics. (What was "Watergate," why did it happen, and what followed from its recognition?)

Plays could be staged, each chosen not only to give students the experience of being on show but also to teach them by experience how to communicate without necessarily using words. Gesture, facial expression, bodily stance—successful politicians have got these talents down well; some even have coaches to prep them in their uses. Such activities will challenge some shy students and others who are embarrassed by the shapes of their bodies. (Start a dance studio and get some older, experienced students to help coach the shy or embarrassed younger classmates.)

Topics such as fear, loathing, embarrassment, exultation, could be assigned to individuals and to small groups of students for them to express the several meanings of each of these words. Many pupils will struggle with this admittedly difficult exercise, and they will have to be helped to get the hang of it. Again, older, experienced students can serve as advisers. Both the neophytes and the coaches can benefit from the experience; many of us, of whatever age and experience, only get deeply into a matter when we have to teach it to another.

Activities such as these take time and careful preparation. They are messy for the teacher: one never knows which class will take to such new assignments with relish and which will not. (Or, even more complicated, which students within the class will grasp what their classmates do not.) Success may even depend on the weather or the day of the week; a snowstorm or a prolonged hot, humid spell can distract even the most dutiful student; a first-period class may be peppy, but a seventh-period class may drag because of the stunning activity demanded in most high schools.

Course planners must take these annoying matters into account, as they cannot be accommodated into a semester-long set of lesson plans. Inexperienced or inattentive teachers may need such crutches, but they are mere palliatives. The inept or distracted teacher needs direction.

2. Measurement and Analysis

The processes of testing, estimating, and gauging by means of mathematics and parallel forms of calculation, and assessment, such as comparison of one object with another

Mathematics, physics, statistics, and visual design are the basic disciplines required here, assuming that these subjects are organized around questions and not merely material to cover.

History supplies many examples. *History* is defined in the *American Heritage Dictionary of the English Language* as "a narrative of events, a story . . . a chronological record of events, as of the life or development of a people or institution . . . an established record or pattern of behavior." Another, less reverent definition puts it aptly: "One of the iron laws of history is that every generation gets to tell the story of the one before it. This can be disconcerting for the generation being put under the microscope of the young 'uns. There probably were old-timers in ancient Greece muttering about how that snotty Herodotus punk got it all wrong" (Don Aucoin, "The Decade of Smoke and Mirrors," *Boston Globe*, November 1, 2008, G26).

How big must an army be to result in a battle worth identifying as historically significant? How about Gettysburg?

How did Lee and Grant assess their likelihoods of success or failure in that battle on the basis of the weaponry and ammunition of 1865? Students can be asked to speculate about these personal assessments on the part of each of those leaders, and then report their findings in class.

How does a society identify a cultural or economic condition worthy of analysis? Is it worthwhile to consider how Franklin D. Roosevelt's administration allotted limited foodstuffs to each of the states, and how individual states divided up their allotments and got them to each affected family? What were the effects of each of those allotments?

A different sort of question, one of long range, is answered by what some scholars might call anthropology or geography: the study of places, what they consist of, and what impact they have on human circumstances. For example, how many years did it take an early ancestor of man to travel up a major south-to-north river? Why did he do it? What did he live on? And how do we know what we know? What new ways of finding out about long-ago times—like carbon dating—have been developed, and where do they lead us?

Many teachers and parents may believe that these sorts of questions are too difficult, and most teachers find that such classes require a good deal of steady, uphill, patient work. Teachers have to be imaginative, and coteaching or team teaching can be useful. Good questions raised by the students may draw on a variety of disciplines, and staff must be available to cope with this worthy challenge.

Another example: a teacher might tie some mathematical problems to a popular issue in social science, say, the presidential elections of 2000 that led to a statistical tie. She might ask the students to analyze the tale of that sort of crisis and then set them the task of role-playing a party leader: What are the options of that leader? Of these, which might be the best to win the primary elections, state by state? Which the nation-wide elections?

Or, referring to an earlier time, a teacher could ask how many men, guns, and rounds of ammunition the Union and Confederate armies consumed at Gettysburg, and how did those data—the wealth of armaments available to each side—explain the actions of Lee and Grant?

The teacher could then move to the immediate action in Iraq: How many American, Iraqi, and allied soldiers devoted to winning that war would it take to achieve that goal (however winning is defined)? What course—there's that word again!—of action would the commanders take? The Shiite commanders? The Sunni commanders? The Kurd commanders? Why might there be differences among the leaders of each of these groups? How do allies (in any sort of work) collaborate? What courses of action might they select? The whole enterprise will move from mathematics to a variety of other ways to determine the answers to these questions, with constant reminders of the deliberate process that is being pursued.

These are complex issues, obviously, and would best be taught in a cross-departmental way, with history and mathematics instructors working in tandem. Some classes whose students are adept in mathematics and aware of the importance of the time involved will need freedom to work out solutions—most productively, perhaps, in small groups. Less skilled students will need more time.

• • •

Projects are messy. They tend to give principals and librarians fits: the arrangements—student by student, teacher by teacher—have to mesh fairly and easily with the demands of other courses. Such coordination is, as a practical matter, only possible in a small school or in a separate "house" within a large school, where a student's special needs and passions are respected. Small is essential, but large is the scope, the respect for thinking, and the engagement that most will summon for the process. My most successful teaching in such an interdisciplinary way was in a "synthesis" course that some colleagues and I taught at Andover. The most compelling subject within that course was hunger. Such a process is "grappling," such as Nancy and I described in *The Students Are Watching*.

These examples remind us of the complexity of school design, the shape of individual courses, and the time required to get the best out of each. It also reminds us that experience—as a teacher and as a scholar—is essential, at least for the core of a team.

Again, so be it. These conditions cannot be escaped. They are what make ours such an exciting profession.

CHAPTER · NINE

Technology

*T*echnology is "the application of science," or so the dictionary instructs us. The uses of technology are varied at work, at home, and in schools. Speech can be part of technology, as in a recording where we or others hear our voices on tape. In this form of communication, vocal cords are the critical tools, more important even than the taping equipment. Lose those cords (say, to cancer), and one loses one's ability to speak directly, but modern technology can help. Engineers have designed sophisticated devices to help victims by producing sounds that resemble speech, allowing that person a modicum of oral communication; however, hearing such people "talk" is upsetting because the sounds, though intelligible, are different than they were earlier. It is difficult not to show our agitation—which then has the result of increasing the self-consciousness of the person with the impairment.

What we have long termed a book is also a form of discriminating art, gathered and sorted by technology. What this implies for planners of the New American High School is that the sources of knowledge available to serve our students are to be found in many places, not just in our classrooms, where we use our voices and describe chalk squiggles on a blackboard but also use audios, videos, and computers. Further, those sources are in constant flux, we hope in accurate and useful forms. Not only do we expect to help our students *receive* these new sources of information; we enable them to express themselves, their information, ideas, and stories in a variety of new forms.

Books are technologies in that they facilitate that communication and send it to a wider world. They provide us messages, whether they are fiction or nonfiction. They are the creations of one or more authors that arise from those writers' sense of what is true and, with fiction, creative. One puts on different spectacles when examining and using each mode. Is the nonfiction true? Is the fiction persuasive? Is a story plausible, or is it beyond the reach of most people's imaginations?

Savvy schools today use all sorts of technologies in their classrooms, from the daily newspaper, delivered to each student at school, to highly sophisticated interactive computer-based problems and lessons. The dictionary is now frequently accessed in digital formats, like an application, and can be instantly revised as new words and ideas enter the language.

High schools—and colleges and graduate schools—lead us through these useful, worthy doors and then abandon us, believing that each of us is ready to go on our own, is able to express what we think or feel in a manner that connects us accurately with what we mean. Because we have learned several new technologies already, with their guidance or on our own, our teachers trust us to handle the challenges to come.

We know these challenges will come, because the world, especially its technology, is in flux. Classical, so-called dead languages, such as Latin, Greek, and Hebrew, are fixed, providing continuity to those who want to find out about the past. Modern languages do not provide as much insight into earlier times, but they keep up with the culture, itself roiling and reflecting a variety of situations and sites. What's more, modern languages can be practiced with real—and interesting—people.

What mastery over technology means in one place will signify something quite different in another. I may use email but will not attempt to send text messages. My elderly thumbs could never manage it! Thus is my communication with my grandchildren enlarged but also at times constrained.

Technology has changed the role of the flesh-and-blood-in-a-classroom teacher. Once the sole authority, he or she has become the director to other sources of knowledge. Libraries are to be consulted, online or in the familiar paper form. A document can be called up on a screen where the whole class can see it. Both students and teachers necessarily become the analysts of ideas, processes, charts, and statistics. Together they can search for the facts and arguments that appear to be cogent and applicable to a particular situation.

Students and teachers can also become searchers, independently or within teams, for new and powerful uses of technology. In these kinds of searches, students often feel a compelling sense of connection with the world outside the school's walls. They also feel as if the product of their own hard mental work may be useful to others. They are beginning to take on a sense of responsibility for the world, more than if they were merely working on a paper to be read by one teacher.

Some examples: the military depends heavily on a variety of technologies. There are devices that can, in a way, see around corners, advising forces of what may be lurking in wait for them. The armies that have such equipment have a great advantage over those that do not. The latter might find themselves suddenly the recipients of shell fire that seemingly comes from nowhere.

Diplomacy depends almost entirely on technology. Much of modern international communication is by means of cable or international telephone communications. Televised or video conversations via Skype are possible over great distances, and the communicators can get some sense of what mood or emphasis each presents. There is dramatic acting in all this; anger or fear can show through. Blogs such as the ones from Israel and South Africa that our granddaughter studies can express bigotry but also a desire to understand one another.

Technology plays a large role in air-traffic control. Flights are given air space and a place in a dependable sequence of take-offs or landings. The success of this routine is measured by its mishaps—which have been virtually nil. One rides his or her flight with few worries, looking out of the small windows and dreaming (once more) of the lay of the land.

On railroads, especially commuter trains, we read our morning papers (or, if younger, do our homework) in the sure belief in the effectiveness of the system. It works, and it has worked now for decades.

Technology has a major role in modern medicine. CT scanners can reveal a full range of pictures of the insides of a person's body quickly and without risk or pain to the patient. The technical description of a CT scanner is "a device that produces cross-sectional views of internal body structure using computerized axial tomography." Few patients (myself included) have any idea of what that definition practically means; suffice it to say, we accept its findings gratefully, even as we must drink a thick white liquid that highlights our innards for the CT scan's production. We can walk away from such a procedure, grateful for its limited, predictable aftereffects. We may not like what we learn, but at least we can be sure of its accuracy.

New books for younger readers are being produced with an accompanying video and video game. The assumption is that the modern reader expects not just to absorb new material but to interact with it. More and more scholarly books in education are also produced with CDs that illustrate the author's ways of reaching her or his conclusions.

What the future will bring is uncertain. At some point hence, we automobile drivers may be able to tune in to an invisible roadside signal that guides us safely at the speed limit, not hitting any other cars or even skidding on unexpected ice—assuming that the roadside signal is programmed to identify slick roads when and where they may appear.

The far future may see further uses of sophisticated technologies. Perhaps each of us drivers will have a sort of PIN that allows us to connect to roadways over which we pass, this allowing us freedom to relax and enjoy the trip. However, I doubt that any technology of whatever merit will give us full confidence in the system; there will always be the chance, however small, of driving errors. A safe driver will be a skeptical driver. As far as I know, a skeptical computer has not yet been invented.

There are other dangers in technology as well. All users of computers must ponder who can invade them (for example, through the spam that appears almost magically). The reader who rushes from a book to a video game may lose the valuable period of thought that a slower process would allow. Another danger for us is to depend too much on technological tools. Just because Google or Wikipedia says something is so, we must never assume that what it tells us is *the* answer or answers. No matter how we receive information, a human being has still provided it. Humans are not always neutral or careful or smart. We must remain cautious, as must our students.

Critics will not like this attitude: "Some things are true—the moon comes up at night, even if we cannot see it through the clouds." To deny that is to confound common sense. Yet we must be wary about most of what is around us, and we must preach the virtues of discrimination and skepticism to all but the youngest of our students. We want them to trust us, but not to believe that everything they are taught and everything they see and hear is automatically true.

Our job must be to find the richest possible assembling of resources to provoke learning in each of our students. This requires, of course, that we know what useful resources are and how they may be harnessed for each student. This will take time and will require collaboration with other teachers and librarians. All of us must also be aware of what technologies are available at home for each of our students and clever in creating assignments requiring the use of these, student by student.

All this is as complicated as it is promising. Behind it all—once again—is the necessity of knowing each student well, how she learns and how she might be changing. The oldest stricture applies to the newest mechanism. How encouraging, especially to an historian!

CHAPTER · TEN

Pedagogy

*P*edagogy is an old-fashioned word. You will not find it used much these days, as it smacks of scholasticism of the worst sort. It comes from the Greek *paidagogia*, meaning a slave who took children to and from school. Pedagogy is also the stock-in-trade of schools of education, those places usually held in low esteem by those both in the classic scholarly disciples and even in supposedly kindred professional schools, such as schools of law, medicine, public administration, and public health. "Pedagogy," implying pretentious but meaningless jargon, has become an epithet in our times.

Whatever the dignity of the word, however, it has— for me at least—a nice, pompous ring to it, giving distinction to my schoolwork. Every worthy high school deserves a pinch of pomp. Moreover, its meaning, the *craft* of teaching, has made me think harder about how my students and I spend our hours together, what I teach, how I teach, and why I teach, and how I might ascertain what is being learned by each student even as the conversation is proceeding. There is analysis here, akin in kind if not in complexity to basic research in any discipline.

I cannot ignore what is likely to be on my students' minds, nor can I shirk my duty to engage them in worthwhile pursuits. Teaching is fundamentally the telling of stories that, one hopes, will take root and continue to grow inside our students' heads. Even mathematics, a logical, progressive discipline—one understanding leads and builds on another— implies movement, the necessity of making sure that the students understand the difference between a line and an area. They are invited to offer what are called "proofs." In writing, they are asked to demonstrate that they understand the difference between reporting and proselytizing. There is analysis in the reading of poetry, in the study of the nature and development of disease, in the basic research involved in every discipline from the physical and social sciences through the arts.

• • •

My introduction to the craft of teaching arose during my two years of active duty in the Army. I had enrolled as a freshman in Yale's Reserve Officers' Training Corps (ROTC)—a decision, I believed, that my father expected and desired. My introduction to carefully designed and delivered information came at Fort Sill, Oklahoma, the Army's field artillery training center. In that sunbaked, sandy place, we were divided into small gun sections and required to put our book learning into action, over and over again. Our duties were to become so ordered that, in time, our learning became habits. This highly focused and endlessly repeated work prepared us well for later work in the field.

Other learning was of an eye-opening nature: an understanding not technical but cultural. We ROTC "college boys" were barracked in dusty wooden buildings, each with a gang shower and bathrooms at the ends. A sergeant, one of our instructors, had a room and a private bath at one end of these World War II buildings. Even when we left this home away from home, we had to keep our backs ramrod straight. Salutes were expected at every turn. We marched in formation everywhere and took grief from regular Army privates as they sped by in trucks; they considered us to be real scum, wet-behind-the-ears pretentious college kids, little naive boys who, someday soon, were going to order them around and then go back to civilian life. Not much respect there. Looking back, I do not really blame them.

The Army was unofficially racially segregated in those days. Blacks were expected to be truck drivers or mess hall workers. The few Asians—mostly South Koreans—who came to Fort Sill for their officer's training also openly mocked us from their trucks as they sped past. They knew from hard experience just what war was.

I learned much on my first assignment in Germany, in the beautiful little town of Schwäbisch-Gmünd, near Stuttgart. I was assigned to be the executive officer of an artillery battery, the "number two" to a captain, in my case a wonderful, wise Texan by the name of William Turley. A career soldier, he took my then twenty-one-year-old self, gave me enormous responsibility, and never seemed to second-guess me. (With five older sisters plus Mum and Anne-Liese, I was used to being second-guessed and considered this a rare occasion!) Immediately, however, Turley put me into the hands of the senior gunnery sergeant, a fellow whom everyone called only by his last name, Haughney, who promptly took me down to the 155 mm howitzers that were our responsibility. The battery's gun mechanic demonstrated how to assemble and disassemble the working parts of the weapon. All this was complicated, and I faked my exhibition of full understanding, believing (wrongly) that he would be deceived. I shudder at that memory to this day, many years hence.

As the "exec," I was required to prepare and oversee all the training, both when in barracks and in the field, for our six howitzer sections. The division required us to work in cycles; as replacement troops arrived, the more experienced troops were expected to lend a hand in training up the newcomers.

With each wave of newly arrived and usually green troops, we were told to "start small," drilling the late teenagers (a few of whom were barely literate) in such matters as how to break up and then reassemble their rifles or carbines. We worked in all kinds of weather and in the dark as well as during the day. We were told to concentrate on the soldiers' routines, making the management of their weapons a deeply set habit so firmly grasped that it seemed almost second nature to express it.

For field exercises, our unit was sent to an old German Army training center to the west at Graffenwöhr, where we could test our ability to fire accurately, and it was there that I learned to train and retrain on the basis of specific evidence: my gun crews threw shells out there into the unseen distance, and these missiles did—or did not—hit their intended targets.

Well-trained crews succeeded at this; sloppy crews made awful, even dangerous, mistakes. This was legitimately nerve-racking, high-stakes work. In those conditions, I watched as the soldiers under my command improved their performance, exceeding their own and my expectations. Indeed, with all that practice, my own performance as their leader improved too.

When our gun sections had the initial skills and habits down, we repeated the exercise, this time as a battery writ large. Officers from the division were assigned to test us, in daylight and at night; each of these tests was ordered without prior warning to any of us, even the battalion commander. If this first testing was persuasively mastered, the examining continued at battalion level and ultimately for the division as a whole. After returning to Schwäbisch-Gmünd, we started the process over again. The lesson for me in all this was that practice was essential, especially when one is learning skills.

In spite of the clear increase in our skills, there was an unreality to all of this, which also pertains to pedagogy. We were part of a so-called regimental combat team that was assigned a sector of the border between us and East Germany, a route that our leaders felt would be hit by the Russians and their Communist allies. We were trained to expect assault by infantry, as in World War I, but our anticipated opponents in the 1950s were most likely to attack with tanks. There was no way our rifles, no matter how quickly assembled, could blunt, much less stop, such an assault. I must admit that this brutal fact somewhat undercut our lessons—and our self-confidence.

I knew how destructive war could be from my father's experience in World War II; he served in the Monuments, Fine Arts, and Archives section in Algeria, Tunisia, and, ultimately Italy. Unfortunately, he suffered a stroke and was sent home. In time he recovered, partly by crafting elegant hooked rugs, also using practice as a way to strengthen his disabled right hand. It delighted me that one of his first rugs was designed as a gift for me, and another shortly afterwards for Nancy when we got engaged just before I left for Germany. Still, his experience during and just after the war had been very hard on him and on the rest of the family, so I knew well that however satisfying it was to improve, our training was not the same as a real war.

My full-time assigned ROTC tour ended, and like my fellow shavetail officers, I rotated out of uniform and went back to civilian life—in my case for our wedding and for my appointment as a teacher of English and mathematics at Boston's Roxbury Latin School. After a year there and another year completing a master of arts in teaching degree at the Harvard Graduate School of Education, I found that more military lessons lay ahead. In 1957, Nancy and I and our newborn son, Tod, traveled to Australia, where I had been offered a job teaching seventh, eighth, and ninth graders English, geography, and history at the Melbourne Church of England Grammar School (MCEGS). I also served as an officer in the MCEGS "cadet corps" and spent a fascinating two weeks with that unit in the Australian Army training ground at Puckapunyal. I was the only non-Aussie officer and was the butt of some good-natured ragging, as I was the "Yank" wearing a "funny uniform."

What I learned from this exercise concerned the level of responsibility that the Australian Army sergeants put on the cadets. The high school students were to move, accurately by compass, in both day and night, and they were kept up for many hours to make sure that they did the right things no matter the circumstances. "You really know something well if you can use it when nodding with fatigue or when distracted," was the explanation for the hard work. "Learning," thereby, was something that was to be so deeply embedded in one's mind that it could be "used" when one was bewildered or inattentive. This military work was to be as second nature— as *habitual*—as the moves on the court of a professional tennis player.

As the last part of my military duty, I enrolled in the Reserves. I attended evening training sessions (at Harvard University's ROTC Center, no less) and was sent with our tiny unit to summer camp at Fort Bragg, North Carolina. Along with some other ragtag Reserve units, we were to serve as an aggressor force to the 81st and 101st Airborne Divisions, which were to be dropped by parachutes and gliders into the fort's many square miles of soft pine forest; they had been instructed to attack our flimsy positions. That the paratroopers were contemptuous of us only emboldened us to shout nasty words in their direction as they played their little game, usually passing us in their jeeps and trucks.

Eventually, I left the Reserves, finding the duties there to be trivial, a sort of club for the officers. There were too few enlisted men to create a unit to command, so we higher-ups spent our evening drill time in a bar. We hoped that the taxpaying public did not know these details about federal service.

• • •

I have not been a soldier since, but at a variety of private, public, and eventually charter schools, I found that the civilian schoolteacher's task could benefit from some aspects of military training. I kept quiet about that belief as so many Americans of that period had negative feelings about military ways and means. However, a number of key elements of pedagogy emerged:

Start small and select a topic that is likely to interest most students but will grow into a broader and more accessible understanding. Begin, say, with a topic such as an important but narrowly contained event like the Battle of Bunker Hill. Take apart its various stages. Learn about the local militias that had been loosely assembled. Attend to the key leaders, especially the arrival of General Washington from his duties in the south and the extraordinary delivery of cannons pulled over snow and ice from Canada by General Gates's volunteers in the nick of time. The British were clearly surprised, and from that event forward, they reckoned that these inexperienced and irregular American militia men could fight well. Thus was the Battle at Bunker Hill a decisive turning point.

Starting small is more likely to engage a student's interest; following a narrative from its local roots to its wider significance will enable a student to grasp the broader concept of a turning point. Understanding why historians make so much of turning points might lead students to understand what "thinking like an historian" actually means.

This can begin at a relatively young age and grow in sophistication over the years. By high school, history students can learn much of the nature of turning points by spotting their emergence, for example, in the revelation of President Nixon's dictation tapes, which led to his resignation. That is, the narrow focus on what at first seemed a small event would give them a concrete example of what a topic—a subject— might be, and would also lead to the more abstract thoughts about the limits of the presidency and the abuse of power.

Past events can illumine a range of conclusions. Take, for example, the story of Eisenhower and his Allied leaders' choice to wear down German morale, not with more frontal blood-shed, but instead by means of a pincer movement, what football aficionados call an unexpected end run. When the Allies showed that Hitler could be attacked from every side, almost with impunity, the fall of the Third Reich followed inevitably. A side effect was to convince Stalin and his Russian armies that Western troops could be smart as well as bold.

Pick the subjects carefully. Subjects must represent a class of influential happenings, not just a one-of-a-kind event. Each must serve as a clear example of what a topic is or might be. Assign writing to the class, asking each student to choose a topic that is of interest to him or her. Some students will balk at this. "Mr. Sizer, I don't know what to write about." Asking them to write a list of what they like to talk about with their friends could jump-start things (though very few are initially interested in, say, Bunker Hill). Another way to evoke a stu-dent's best work would be to relate the topic to his own story. Press him with questions. "Where did your parents grow up?

Were their early, school-going years like yours are now, or were they different? If those years were different, why was that so?"

Treat the students like the adults they are becoming. Soak them in both experience and in the actual documents—the collected facts of a time, the facts that gave body to a subject. Some of these documents should be familiar—the Declaration of Independence, for example—but some should be unexpected. "Why not write a piece about the Patriots coach Bill Belichick and his alleged 'spying' on the signals used by the Pats' opposing teams? Did other coaches 'spy'? Was Belichick the only one to use this ruse? Would that make any difference? What are all the facts of the case? What are the different rules and mores that need to be considered in such a decision?" Inspire them, if you can; inspiration helps them remember ideas and knowledge.

Like the young soldiers who practiced taking apart their weapons, my students since have been asked to demonstrate their mastery both of the content of those documents and of their meaning. Time in class has been used for these important activities, and feedback has been offered and gratefully accepted, but in the name of practice rather than high stakes. These simulations have been their tests.

• • •

Pedagogy—taking the time to consider what helps students learn—forces an educator, first, to explain to himself or herself why we do what we do when we have students in class. For example, why are most secondary schools designed the way they are? Is it for convenience? If so, whose convenience? If we educators are essentially concerned with what the students learn rather than merely what they are presented, how do we decide what is more or less important for these particular students at this particular time?

Should we try to connect what students learn outside school with what we teach? How should we use—and cope with—the media? In many homes, the TV is on virtually all the time, watched some of the time, ignored most of the time. It provides sights, sounds, and words that are often considered a soothing background for the activity of a busy household. Of course, the media are not the only distractions that settle into a family as it matures. Our students may have a passion for music and sports, both as players and as fans; they may take trips and have hobbies. One of my principal "distractions" these days are birds; Nancy and I live in some woods where the banks of high oaks protect the smaller avian species from hawks looking for their dinner. We waste early morning hours just watching them while drinking coffee.

What does this sort of pleasant activity (from listening to music to watching birds) have to do with pedagogy? It exemplifies the reality that we learn (are taught) all the time and that, say, learning and enjoyment are useful outcomes of watching, of pondering what it means, for birds and for humans, to be alive, and of pondering whether birds have souls.

Any New American High School should encourage its students to get into the habit of watching and listening to all that is going on around them, the gentle and cruel, the totally familiar and the surprisingly new alike. We must set up assignments that will require our students to take risks; coping with the previously unknown is an essential habit for the educated person of whatever age. The elements of that process—watching, listening, sensemaking as a matter of habit—can come together to create a powerful pedagogy.

Trying to take in many sensations at once, however, might interfere with the focus that is also a central part of learning.

"I'm taking an extra load this spring, five instead of four," a student tells me. "Good for you," I comment. "Is there a special course you want to take? Do you plan to graduate early?" My not-so-hidden message: energy is good, but there has to be a good reason to take on extra work, and often less is more.

"Maybe I will," he replies. "We all need the credit from sixteen courses. I may be able to do it in three years plus a summer." Once again we see serious learning reduced to what is measurable in an exquisitely calibrated sense. The penny-bank system of education is difficult to change; it is in all our bones. That is why the conversations between students, teachers, and parents at the Francis W. Parker Charter Essential School, where students control the pace at which they go through the curriculum, are so extensive and deliberative.

Or maybe we teachers should worry less about what and how *we* teach and more about how we encourage our students to understand their own learning—and thus, we hope, teach *themselves*. Margaret Metzger, a veteran high school teacher, told us recently that when she was in high school, a definite focus for all of her teachers was on a separate section at the end of each assignment, in which each student was asked to describe exactly what she had learned and how she had learned it. Over four years in high school, answers grew more sophisticated, from "I read the assignment," to "I paid attention to the topic sentences," to "I discovered that sometimes a topic sentence comes later in the paragraph." Margaret said that they were not graded on how they answered the questions, but that over time, and without overt competition, they came to value the growth, not only in the learning itself but also in their own effectiveness as learners. She believes that it was the greatest lesson she learned in high school.

Not many schools are as determined and consistent as that high school, but many these days work on the task of helping their students know themselves as learners. In this way, students who read quickly can guard against being sloppy; those who read slowly can pay attention to the cues that will indicate where they are going. All can acknowledge their level of engagement and how it affects their learning. *Do I learn only what mirrors my previous experience? or my prejudices? How can I stay attentive when I feel that what I am being taught is over my head? or is something with which I disagree?*

Answering these questions involves pedagogy in the broadest sense.

• • •

Pedagogy logically is a subject for which schools of education are—or should be—responsible. It all depends, of course, on how those schools define pedagogical skill. Is pedagogy merely the training necessary to contribute to a penny-bank system of schooling?

Is teaching more a science than an art? Is sophisticated teaching the instruction of ideas and skills, matters of speaking and telling? That is, can we describe the steps a teacher must make, ultimately as a matter of habit, in enough detail to allow careful testing to determine whether the work has succeeded?

To my eye, teaching—pedagogy—is an art and, thus, practiced as an art, the arts of telling and listening, a process that moves back and forth, silently or audibly, between the learner and the book or orchestra or band or television program. Pedagogy assumes reciprocity.

It also requires engagement, and that means it must center on topics that are relevant to the students and on important problems about which they want to be clear in their own minds. To create an environment of engagement, one cannot always rely on the obvious high stakes of the battlefield. One must depend on a student's imagination and farsightedness. There is trial and error.

Central to my pedagogy was the asking and answering of questions. This was designed not as a "gotcha" exercise (Did you do the homework? If so, you will provide the one obvious answer) but as a way of establishing an ever-deepening dialogue, one in which a variety of answers might be acceptable and even helpful. A topic is selected, such as the Korean War. "Who started it?" you ask. The conventional answer would be "the North Koreans."

You counter, "But why did the northerners attack?"

"They were starving."

You push back: "Starving for what? Food? Iron ore?" The students say, "Yes." You add, "Might they have been starving for *freedom*?" A smart kid parries, "It depends on how you define 'freedom' . . . like *Freedom from Want, Freedom from Fear*, Franklin Roosevelt's 'Four Freedoms.'"

What about freedom from doubt? Freedom from worrying about the spread of communism? Freedom from worrying about finding and holding a job? Freedom from worrying about making the "right" choices for a mate? The joust goes on, especially because the subject matter edges so close to the students' personal but rarely expressed concerns.

There is danger here. A student or a parent might complain that dialogue about one's personal freedoms—or worries—has no place in a public school classroom. It is an invasion of privacy, and, they might feel, it assaults a parent's or clergyman's domain. Or a teacher may say that this kind of lesson is too much like preaching or therapy and is inappropriate in a public school classroom. A district or state official might complain that time spent on such abstractions takes the students' eyes off their upcoming state or College Board tests.

These concerns have merit. Questions can seem nosy and freewheeling; discussion of important personal and social topics does invade test-prep schedules. This moves the issue to the policy arena. If plumbing social topics is indeed important—it certainly was fifty years and more ago—why aren't these topics given time and importance within the formal program of a school? Why, indeed.

The issue then starts climbing the educational hierarchy. If such matters as decency, honesty, social justice, and each student's effort to determine her individual values are indeed important, why not spend time on them? Finally, how to test such topics, in the best sense? If you have no idea whether your students have learned from their discussions, have you been wasting their time? Yet multiple-choice, machine-graded tests, however legitimate in other areas, will not work here. What to do?

Turn to the humanities and the arts, subjects that require assessment that is apt and fair. Carefully phrase the expected standards, insofar as that is possible. Describe your work to a panel of judges and tell them how you might assess it. Take care not to devalue the process, somehow reducing it to a simplistic matter.

Simply take careful note of what and how you teach, classroom by classroom, age group by age group, student by student, and try to find the most useful approach for each. Go over your class lists periodically, asking yourself how you are doing with each student. Compare your judgments with another teacher of the same students. Are we both seeing the same student? Are we teaching him or her in an appropriate way? Are different ways appropriate for different subjects, or for the same subjects at a different time?

All this sort of professional activity requires time to pursue it and a small school or a human-scale autonomous unit within a large school. It is hard to teach well—to be a worthy *pedagogue*—when you are stuck with a whirl of students, coming and going, for whom you have not even a sure sense of their names and what each would prefer to be called, let alone what their particular challenges are.

Pedagogy requires focus, and focus requires order, yet *order* is often a threatening word. "We teachers had better get this business of ours into good order, or we will be in BIG trouble," I-the-principal tell my colleagues. Hierarchies make things easier for us educational bureaucrats. He reports to her. She reports to them. They report to me. We design our schools as orderly hierarchies, on the assumption that the higher the authority, the more certain he or she is that this is the way things are, the truth. It's all very orderly—at least in the school manual.

Order is defined in a dictionary as "a comprehensible arrangement," and to be effective, a school must be orderly. *No running in the hallway.* No clever exceptions in rules or expectations that might give us cause to forgive you for your sins.

Yet the definition does not do justice to a complicated concept. Why did Abraham Lincoln, just after finishing a tragic war whose primary purpose was to restore order, refuse to arrest General Robert E. Lee? May there be some *forgiveness* in *order*? In our desire to teach our students to be orderly and predictable, are we imposing on them a steadfastness that might grow inappropriate over time?

The painful fact is that learning, and thus schooling, must at times be *disorderly*. Young people are in the process of change in everything from their bodies to their minds to their aspirations (or lack of aspirations). They flop around, strut a bit, and are hilarious for us to watch as they try to act—and be—"grown up." Of course, we must never show our delight in their thrashings around; we went through that stage too and may remember its agonies. Even the floppy, unwashed, and cursing kid deserves some respect (as well as a request that he clean up his body and his act).

Effective schools not only accept this reality but create order, changing the dimensions of that order as conditions require. The irony and paradox is that to be truly orderly, a school must be—assuredly will be—disorderly. A quiet student is not necessarily a thinking student. He must ask some questions, express some differences, in order to engage with ideas.

Furthermore, the subjects of the curriculum are in constant evolution as findings from research become available. Textbooks lag in revisions, making a teacher's job more difficult. We ask our students, "What have you learned when you compare recent findings about space from the Internet with what your text says? Not everything on the Web is true! Knowledge must be around for a while to be validated. But not everything in your textbook may be true either, or true anymore!"

For teachers, order and the related notion of faith are two sides of the same coin. We need assurance that some things are what we are told they are, that there is an order to the world. At the same time, we must recognize that this commitment is an act of faith, faith in the care and precision of the men and women who do research and tell us what they have found. We must accept, however, the fact that some researchers get it wrong or that new findings in a related field challenge some things in which we have had faith. A thinking people must be ready to keep open minds.

In schools, much give and take over these issues takes place in meetings. In 1915, a West Point graduate named Hubert Robert drew up some rules to be used in debates; they have survived intact to this day and are, appropriately, called Robert's Rules of Order. They have become a guide by which discussions and debates are pursued. Their acceptance is remarkably widespread, though a recent book, *Roberta's Rules*, provides some modifications that are more appropriate for meetings that include both men and women.

The flaw in the whole notion of providing rules to ensure order is evident, but usually repressed: What is order? Do rules apply to conditions, or only to meetings? Who has the right to define order for the world? Does the word mean the stable, orderly condition that will allow for international peace? The assumption that it does is reflected in the early confidence placed in the victors of World War II and in the United Nations and its Security Council. Many world history textbooks display the photograph of President Roosevelt, Prime Minister Winston Churchill, and Marshal Josef Stalin at the Crimean resort community at Yalta. Roosevelt's polio-crippled legs are front and center, with a smiling Stalin on one side and a Churchill looking like a bulldog on the other. That photograph alone can be used as the springboard for lively class discussions in senior high schools. Can three old and exhausted men guarantee order, no matter how powerful their nations, how carefully their agreements are worded or their institutions are structured? What happens when power is shared more widely? How can the benefits of order be sustained over time?

Many teachers grade tests on a 0–100 scale. This is orderly, even accepted, though it seems more understandable in some fields, such as mathematics, than in others, such as poetry.

Students may not like tests in the first place, but if they take them, they want to know how they did. I well remember how angry our son was when his chemistry teacher, trying to counter what he called his students' obsession with grades, refused to tell them whether or not he was grading on a scale of 0–100. "Then don't give a grade," grumbled our son—to us, not to him. "But what am I supposed to do with this 73 when I don't know whether it's out of 75 or 200?"

For teachers, there are all sorts of approaches to "keeping order," some wonderfully described by Kathleen Cushman in her book *Fires in the Bathroom: Advice for Teachers from High School Students*. If someone gathers some paper towels and puts a match to them, just to see what happens, that is clearly disorder, and the students interviewed by Cushman were grateful for the help that adults could give in restoring order again. Still, they insisted, this help was to be offered carefully and with respect.

Teachers often feel that schools are asked to socialize or even civilize their students, but *civilized* will be a hard word for most teenagers to swallow. It carries the baggage of self-righteousness, and most adolescents despise the self-righteous adult. It cannot be avoided, however; when people of any and all ages gather, there have to be rules of discourse and conduct: that is what civilization is all about.

Order is not the main goal. We should attend to order, but sensitively—and not too much. Teachers and students should not be servants of a rigidly predictable clock and bell system. Furthermore, schools must not only *be* civilized places. They must actively press their occupants to observe and ponder the nature of such places in order to learn from them, warts and all. We expect our children to learn the value of safety and that peaceful, constructive communities do not just happen; they are created by people who care about the common weal. Finally, as they grow older, we expect them to take a role in that creation and re-creation of such communities, from teams to choruses to student councils. This is the dynamic, but often somewhat disorderly, process that competent adults use when changes must be made.

A school's design has a large impact on the pedagogy that will be used in it. A sound pedagogical strategy will take time. Other matters supposedly covered will have to be dropped. Each student, of whatever precocity, will be on his or her own track, and each will have to have his or her own learning plan, much like the ones created every year for every student at the Parker School. The school's overall curriculum will have to shrink to provide for this focus. Simplicity and focus for everyone must become the norm.

• • •

In sum, teaching is first and foremost a demanding art. There is science to it (just as with painting) but also *style*, the quality of a person's actions whether that person is fifteen or fifty. Getting others to learn, which includes helping them acquire skills, is a subtle, complex business, especially as no two people learn in precisely the same way, and no one person may learn in the same way over time, even with similar subject matters. This is a happy fact, actually: each of us is affected by time and place, and, in this new context (which may be nothing more than after a good night's sleep), the person may "get it" in a way that she could not the day before.

Pedagogy depends on a teacher's character, his experience, his willingness to examine what is going on in his classes and to test his judgments against those of others. It requires self-confidence and a willingness to listen to the views of others. Those of us in education must accept this inevitable fuzziness and learn how to live with it as artists do.

CHAPTER · ELEVEN

Testing

*A*ssessment is part of life: necessary, constant, and subject to revision, thus relatively gentle. *Evaluation* is in that neighborhood, though like assessment, its meaning centers around standards—or values—that need to be known and understood by the person being evaluated in order for him or her to approach the process confidently and bravely. *Measurement* is beginning to be fearsome; if measured, one is subject to the idea that at a certain point in time, one will be compared to others and might not measure up. And *testing* is a strong, often threatening word. It puts one up to a challenge. It gives each of us a gauge, a more or less standard means of determining what we and our students have done. At its most extreme, such as the SATs, it is also seen as indicating not only what one has done but also what one can do.

First, we need to make clear the distinctions between testing ourselves, being tested by others whom we know well, and, finally, being tested by people whom we don't know and—even more important—who don't know us. Technically defined, a test is a "procedure for critical evaluation; a means of determining the presence, quality, or truth of something; a trial." The *Random House Dictionary* tells us that it is "something accomplished successfully, especially by means of exertion." Although testing has always been part of schooling, in recent years it has come to dominate the curriculum, the schedule, and the relationships that need to work well for real learning to exist. Thus you need to consider this process more broadly and deeply before you make any specific plans for your high school.

Testing can be fun. It can be disguised as play. It is a way to check things out, to try alternatives. With others' help, we find ways to test ourselves, stretching our ability to push ahead or handle difficulties, to demonstrate our endurance. Many ambitious kids want to test their mettle. Are they good enough to satisfy themselves? Only after they have learned something do they want to show off for those who observe them.

Testing ourselves seems to be hardwired into our psyches. A tiny baby will reach for her toy again and again, and when she is able to grasp it, smiles with satisfaction. She has progressed; she has accomplished something, and she knows it. A person often chooses to be tested, albeit by herself. Nancy's needlework is a good example of that self-imposed testing; she must gauge carefully the color and length of the yarn she needs for each small step in the creation of a piece of work, such as an individualized tag to use as a key chain or a little block that she makes for newborn babies in our extended family or for friends. (The cheekier of the new parents let her know as soon as a birth has taken place that she had better get her needle flying! Our family and friends curiously run to twins, thereby requiring a pair of blocks. Fortunately, no close young relative or friend has come up with quintuplets yet!) If something that Nancy has made doesn't look right, there is no one to tell her to do it again, but she usually does.

A different form of testing involves another person: parent or teacher or employer or coach. It is a person who wishes you well, who plans to help you succeed, but who needs to push you out of your comfort zone, sometimes quite firmly. A coach tests his players by putting them into awkward positions, such as five on two when training a lacrosse team. A father puts his life in the hands of an inexperienced but practicing driver. (Because I was a sixth child, my father was given dispensation from that duty, and it fell to a newly married brother-in-law to perform that ritual. I remember him as forbearing but tough on me as he made me change gear after gear on a number of hills.) An employer such as the parent of little children puts a teenager in charge of guaranteeing health and safety while she is away. All hope, of course, that the teen won't be "put to the test" with an accident or an intruder, but parents do depend on teenagers to be capable and mature no matter the circumstances. These kinds of tests are individual; rarely is one timed or compared with others; the goal is only to increase one's skill or to perform well in completing an assigned task. "I am definitely becoming a better writer," a Parker student told me. Athletes often call it one's "personal best."

Teachers often use the word "test" or else the less frightening word "assessment." Testing is what we teachers do to ascertain whether each of our students has mastered the content and skills of that which we have required and offered. We call all this "achievement." If we do not know what each child has mastered—and has mastered so well that it is likely to stick with him or her—how can we decide what and how to teach, and for how long? How else can I teach each child most appropriately?

Tests are important. The students feel as though they are on the line, similarly to when they are writing a paper but far more than when reading a chapter. If you ask a kid what his homework is, he will mention his tests first. If you ask him how school is, he'll tell you that he did well on a recent test. Or, for obvious reasons, he won't.

Most teachers do what they can to make their tests fair. The classic American definition of the word *testing* uses the notion of a known and predictable procedure, an action that requires patience and implies movement. This is best achieved in the classroom, where the teacher knows what work the students have been asked to do and what discussions have taken place over a certain length of time. The test can be given when the students are ready for it, and not before. There are valid reasons for testing that even the students acknowledge, though testing in schools is rarely seen as a benign undertaking.

At times, out of insecurity, distraction, or laziness, tests are designed and used as a crutch. There is "being testy" too, being irritated, impatient, or exasperatingly peevish (as the *Random House Dictionary* puts it). The *Oxford English Dictionary* goes further and puts action into the word: headstrong, obstinate. The testy kid can make a teacher impatient and frazzled. "What are we going to do with him? He stalls on everything as soon as I talk with him. What an unlikable kid, at least today." Of course, teachers can get testy too, especially at test time.

Other tests, such as those for emotional intelligence, are more personal and individualized, according to Daniel Goleman, who has studied and written about many aspects of this subject. Can we cope with disappointments, such as having to cancel a long-planned trip to a place that we enjoy in order to stay close to a grieving neighbor? Can we find a morsel of good in bad situations? Can we find ways to deal with what he calls "emotional hijacking" and the resulting inability to think?

Some of the most common emotional tests are also the most subtle, such as those I-the-teacher use on myself almost instinctively from the moment my students cross the threshold of my classroom. How well have I introduced my students into the culture of learning? Do they have their books with them? Do they look me in the eye? If they don't, what might they be holding back?

Do some of them crowd around others, whispering "What did you get on that problem?" "How do you do this one?" Is their conversation a form of collaboration, or is it pretending to have done something they have not done? I will inevitably see both the good and the venal in this ancient and persistent practice. I remind myself that there are many ways that students can learn. Competition can be helpful, but it is more often overdone. Indeed, most of what they learn, for good or ill, emerges from their lives beyond the organized school system. How they learn, too.

The examples I've given so far are all tests of oneself or tests by people with whom we have a relationship. Being assessed is never easy and is often hard to accept, but its purpose is usually understandable. The most problematic—and rampant—form of testing today is that which is devised and graded outside our classrooms and even our schools. We find ourselves being tested not only by ourselves but by others, by our defenders and our critics, by our parents and by state and federal governments. Students, teachers, administrators, schools, even school systems are being evaluated all the time. And the stakes are high.

Of course, there are high-stakes tests beyond the schoolroom. As I have discussed, military units are frequently tested in the field at war. How often have we heard of battle-tested members of the First Cavalry Division successfully capturing a key town in Iraq? A corps of reporters comes up with such language, carefully monitored by military censors. Reading about these soldiers in our comfortable living rooms, we are grateful for their rigorous training and experience. Unfortunately, many of these people are required to come up with only the successful events—where the troops met the challenge of their test—ones that put them in a good light. "Failed" tests are far less likely to be reported, save by the most clever and persistent questioners.

This third form of testing—standardized ostensibly in order to be objective and efficient—is widespread but controversial today. Colleges have long used standardized tests to determine which students they should admit, though the tests' importance in the decision varies. In recent years, governments have used tests to see if the standards of achievement that we have required of each student or groups of students have been "delivered"—at least if we agree on just what might be meant by successful delivery.

External tests are frequently focused on a body of ideas and skills that a local school system, the state or federal government, or a private or church authority deems to be important. Do those authorities understand the wise flow of the classroom? Most do not and cannot, if the rigid and expensive assessment systems they have chosen to use are any indication. As a result, there are really different conceptions of the best and most reliable form for finding out what the student knows—the from-the-top tests and those that good teachers use to find out just what and how each student learns. For most of us teachers, the reality of top-down tests' taking precedence over our assessments is galling, a rebuke to our professional competence, even to our academic freedom.

Another bad side of these standardized tests—arrogantly called "instruments of mastery" by the powerful testing companies—is that if they are not sensitively presented, they can so terrify a student that she or he simply shuts down, paralyzed with fear. A classroom that is filled with fear is a place that teaches students to keep their heads down and try to be invisible, a poor result with ramifications far beyond the immediate situation. Still another bad side of all this testing is its expense—for example, in Ohio in 2007, $82 million was spent on standardized testing, a high school principal from the Buckeye State told me. "What assessments we could have designed with all that money!"

The federal government, which for decades had attempted to help poor students by diverting special money to the areas in which they lived, in 2007 attempted to use test scores as a way to determine whether the districts were making good use of such governmental largesse. Republicans, who tend to be suspicious of federal spending, liked it because they liked to know that money wasn't being wasted. Democrats liked it because they appreciated that more money was being spent on districts populated by poor children. Testing, both sides claimed, would provide federal and state policymakers with an inexpensive, impressive benchmark of the achievement of each child, thus revealing which professionals were more—or less—successful in promoting the progress of each student and therefore of his or her school. The so-called No Child Left Behind Act of 2007 is the key federal expression of this policy. States also have developed, or are developing, their own evaluations; our state has the Massachusetts Comprehensive Assessment System, MCAS for short. (The word *comprehensive* is a tad scary: Does it imply that public servants can test any or all of us on any or all topics, from whether we drive within the speed limit 100 percent of the time to whether we brush our teeth daily or change bed sheets every fortnight?)

MCAS, like other standardized tests, drives curricula and has spawned "test prep" companies that, for a substantial fee, prepare kids for the ordeal that looms before them. The questions were devised by committees of teachers, but are to be administered to all children, no matter what curriculum is in place at their schools. The emergence of the controversial history questions in the spring of 1999 led two teachers from the Francis W. Parker Charter Essential School, where Nancy and I were acting co-principals, to the statehouse in Boston, where they offered legislators, their staff members, and passers-by the chance to take a short test (drawn from MCAS history samples), supposedly to reassure them that the policies they were pursuing were fair and sound benchmarks by which to judge students and the schools they attended. This assignment was met with shock and embarrassment by the state officials, most of whom avoided our colleagues, instead sending aides from their office staffs, if anyone. Those who did take the tests were chagrined by their apparent incompetence in handling facts, suppositions, and opinions in a sure and accurate manner. Or was it, perhaps, that such information, relying on memorization, did not seem relevant in later years?

What teachers know—and what those who do not teach, including journalists and politicians, seem to forget—is the obvious fact that no two of their students learn in precisely the same way at the same time. Most of the students may appear to have a grasp of the general thrust of a topic, but what it *means* to them when they put it into action will differ. One student may remember the politics of the situation (say, Franklin D. Roosevelt selling the New Deal to Congress), but others will recall only juicy tidbits (say, the fact that Eleanor Roosevelt was Franklin D. Roosevelt's distant cousin). We need to get good data in order to plan instruction, student by student. Getting that data is frustratingly time-consuming and often confusing, and there will be no inexpensive shortcuts.

What appeals to me as a teacher is a mix of approaches, each requiring both hard work and open minds from the adults who serve our children.

The task for school designers is to come up with a variety of tests (sometimes airily termed "assessment instruments") that can be used to assist the teachers in understanding their students, to inform parents and guardians, and to provide the state with data that could give them a sense of the academic progression of each child.

Each of us teachers should keep a log of how each student is doing—that is, mastering the material on the time schedule of the school. We should refer back to the apparent progress of each student and figure out if any changes are needed to adjust to where each student is. Carefully and imaginatively, we should adapt the district's demands to who our students are and where in their development in our subjects they appear to be.

"We couldn't do that," teachers and principals might say. "It would take too much time." However, they should take note of the fact that medical doctors do this as a matter of basic practice: they ask, "What are this patient's apparent symptoms? Can I trust him to be honest with me about himself, not sliding off by telling me what he may think I should hear or what he hopes I should hear in order to give him an 'easy' regimen?"

Each teacher should consult with members in other departments about a worrisome student, and consider whether he or she needs special arrangements or special help, such as tutoring. Teachers of English or a foreign language may use quite different, but in each case very appropriate, instruments. Teachers should also be willing and able to describe to those teachers who will inherit the student both the developments and the challenges that she faced.

Of course, all this individual attention plays hob with classroom dynamics, the need to keep order among rampant differentiation, and a school's schedule and expectations. It will slow things down and upset the expected uniform march toward term's end. But is there any work more important in the long run?

At the Parker School, assessment is most clearly seen in the form of what are called gateways. Students enter the school when they have completed grade 6, but they progress through the three divisions of the school at varying rates. Curriculum there is seen in the form of a two-year package that emphasizes the skills and content most appropriate to a middle and high school education. Some may master the Division I work in less than two years, others in more than two; it is up to the student. For example, Susan in Division I in the arts/humanities domain may have been doing work in a variety of areas—such as critical reading, creative writing, oral presentation, and others—that meet her teachers' expectations for work she will be asked to do in Division II. She actually has been graded with a number of "Meets" and even an "Exceeds" or two in the upper right-hand corner of her papers, and she hasn't had a "Just Beginning" or an "Approaches"—the other two grades—in months. She collects all her Meets work in a portfolio as evidence of her teachers' confidence that she is ready to move into the more demanding division. She writes a cover letter for her portfolio, making her case not just in terms of intellect but in terms of her maturity and emotional resilience as she takes up more demanding work with new and usually older students. If her parents and her teachers, most especially her adviser, believe that she is ready to do Division II work, a gateway is arranged.

I used to joke about these gateways, and especially about how quickly the noun became a verb, as in "I am determined to gateway by the end of this year." But at Parker they are serious business. Gateways are what we believe our students must undertake in order to display the results of their schooling. These are how we judge the learned skills, the familiarity with material, and the ability to apply what they know to solving problems. These are a fair and sensitive way to promote those who have met goals, who demonstrate the deepest understanding of the assigned and expected work. They also most tellingly imply, however, the need for flexibility in means, child by child, as they meet a focused common standard.

Gateways are offered twice a year, necessitating much planning, hard work, and even readjustments when they indicate that a candidate has bitten off more than she can chew. Although the process is designed so that there are few unwelcome surprises, the students and their parents (and grandparents, siblings, friends, and neighbors!) are justifiably cautious, even nervous. At the gateway, students are invited to speak about subjects that they know well, but they are also asked questions and, most important, follow-up questions. At the end, as the student is invited into the next phase of her education, the relief and pride are palpable. In each gateway, into Division II and then Division III, the questions are more difficult, the planning more autonomous, until Exhibition at the end of her final year guarantees the student's diploma.

This word "Exhibition" was used at Phillips Academy from its earliest days as an indication that its graduates could demonstrate publicly their proficiency in Latin and Greek. Requirements have broadened since then, and there are too many graduates to perform; we in the audience have to take their teachers' word for the fact that the graduates are ready for the challenges that lie ahead. At the Parker School, however, we can still go to Exhibitions and see for ourselves. We might even take the opportunity to ask one of the questions, making ourselves an important part of the testing process.

• • •

There is, finally, another part of the argument about evaluation: Why test at all? Is not the delivery of skills and content a virtue unto itself?

Or, how much is enough? Why do we have to check? Of course there is the story of the farmer who rushed out every morning to pull on his stalks of corn, and don't you remember how angry your mother got when you peeked in the oven to see how the chocolate cake was baking? Opening that door (thereby introducing a rush of air into the stove) might make the cake sink, losing its fluffiness and thereby wasting a fine afternoon snack. There is a danger in too much measuring; even teachers would agree. Still, they are likely to reply that school practice is considerably more complicated than baking a cake. And their critics are likely to be pressuring them to provide more measurement rather than less. Furthermore, in our age with its obsession for transparency, they seek information that is simple to understand, not full of the individualism and nuance that true professionals require.

The whole idea of measurement of every matter that might affect people is flawed. Why do we have to know everything that is happening as we grow up—and eventually as we grow "down"? Testing has become a modern fetish. There's too much of it around, too much arrogance on the part of those who insist on the tests, too much confidence in the results of such tests. When (say) government thinks it has the duty (no less) to find out about our learning on the basis of a threadbare procession of sterile examinations, an arrogance emerges that has no place in a free society.

Who has the right to test us, anyway? There is an ethical issue here. The medical community has some sense of that; the tests that I have at the hospital are held in strict and protected confidence, to be shared only with the express permission of my doctor and me. I-the-patient understand the need for tests, and welcome them. We want our physicians to know everything that can be known about what ails us. Yet even though our bodies are basically similar to each other—more similar than our minds, at least—most doctors feel that their "readings" of the tests need to be informed by other aspects of our health that don't show up on the tests. Instead of following a rigid list of "standardized" treatments, they start by evaluating where we are in physical health and intellectual strength and build onward from there. They help us the most when they take us one by one. Might that not be true of teachers too?

However, in our sensible New American High School, the leaders have to know at least the basics about how each of its students is faring and how healthy the institution is collectively. Without such checking in, we cannot make useful adjustments.

Let us make those adjustments, but very carefully. Let us pay careful deference to the wishes of each child's family. Let us intervene only when there is clear evidence of inadequate learning on the child's part. Even as we intervene, family members should have a right of appeal. Let us make this loosely policed freedom not only a right but the norm. And let us develop, analyze, and redevelop the external tests that appear accurately and fairly to indicate each student's mastery of the core intellectual skills of literacy, mathematics, and civic understanding, leaving the teachers inside the schools the jobs of assessing the success of the rest of the curriculum.

An educational approach that depends ultimately on a variety of assessment procedures will puzzle many citizens. I only ask them to be fair in their analysis: Which system of formal education makes the greater sense: one that is imposed—with the best of intentions—in a uniform and bureaucratic way, or one that arises from the individuality and informed preferences of individuals?

Let's test in the schools, but do so carefully both in what we ask the students to display to us and what meaning that has for each of those students, one by one. Let us give the students tests that represent plausible situations, ones that connect the teenagers to the world they know. Put them into a familiar situation: "Does it make a difference if I buy six hockey pucks for $6.00 or one at $2.00 every time I lose one?" "If Simon, our regular third baseman, hits over .300 in today's game, what are the chances that he will hit the ball tomorrow when he is called off the bench as a pinch hitter?" "Shall I sign up for a regular weekly lunch at the school's cafeteria or make my own lunch day by day from foods that I buy at the grocery store?" What criteria are important to me? Money? Time at home or in school?

Let us get into the habit of discussing tests and test results within faculty groups; the different meanings will readily emerge here. As we learn more about them, we may be able to modify them, accept them, or at least prepare for them. Heads in the sand are not going to help anyone.

Let us make sure that parents and guardians know why we are testing and what those examinations include. Despite your misgivings about some aspects of the tests, don't give the adults the feeling that their children's time is being wasted.

Let us be patient. Even the weather can slow us down: a heat wave can be an immediate distraction. This means that we must be flexible. Because humans learn differently, not all of us can or should get to the same place at the same time. Yes, we must push when appropriate. But there must be alternatives from among which our students, with our agreement, can select.

For example, can one student, a youngster who is fascinated by different sorts of people, best study the New Deal by reading various speeches, commentaries, and biographies about Roosevelt? Can another start with all sorts of data, including paintings, even the design of post offices produced by WPA-supported artists?

What can a student learn from movies? Music? Narratives? How can he learn to translate what he has learned from one domain—such as these post office artists—into language that will help explain it to another group, such as politicians?

Or perhaps students can study what we are trying to understand on their behalf: tests. Perhaps they can start with the simple word and figure out the various meanings that might be applied to it. By finding examples of assessment that were required in the New Deal, either by uncovering actual information or imagining likely scenarios, they will gain, one hopes, both perspective and a respect for the power of language.

• • •

Few basic American businesses work—at least work well—on a rigid system. For example, a big snowstorm means many fewer families going to the grocery store, so managers must put vegetable and fruit stocks previously presented into refrigerators. Or a garage may have a surge of people wanting chains put on, so extra people have to be hired.

Flexibility is a virtue. For best results, we teachers must know when to test, whom to test, and why. Only with optimal conditions can we test with a reasonable degree of accuracy. It is, of course, easier merely to take some old exam that you have used before, brush it off, and use it once again, but for at least a few students, that approach will backfire. Patience and humility will always be required, even of the veteran teacher in a highly scripted school. Indeed, it is the veteran who is most likely to be aware of the cautions that are necessary in the use of the tool of testing.

And then let what we thus have learned be put quickly to use in support of each child's progress.

CHAPTER · TWELVE

Choice

The role of choice in the New American High School must be considered in ways both broad and historical, for at its core, choice is an important expression of democracy. By definition, freedom implies choice. In local, state, and national governments, elections provide the voters with choices, save in districts where (for example) an incumbent is the only name on the ballot, where opponents believe that raising the money and devoting the time to a campaign would not be worthwhile. This is realistic on their part, and less expensive, but it is also a shame.

One can see choice in action in the deliberations and decisions of the nation's Supreme Court in Washington. Although some courts have been uncontroversial, the justices being so very like-minded, sometimes even graduates of the same law school, others have been divisive, contentious, and at times petty. In the end, each consults his or her own opinion, and decides.

Dissents, and even different versions of an assent or a dissent, are recorded, studied, and cited decades later. Whatever the stresses, however long it takes, individual freedom in a democracy is crucial to the American Way.

There are sensible exceptions. As in our Pledge of Allegiance, we tend to want to pair "liberty and justice for all." The liberty part appeals to most everyone; justice is a little more problematic. We also want to get things done as a community and a body politic, so all these worthy goals need to make allowance for each other, which has the effect of reducing choice.

Almost all analysis involves choice. Good lawyers listen carefully to the issues that are brought to them. They take notes about what concerns the client. They pull all this together and ask for the necessary time to look for analogous cases and precedents. They ultimately present these and ask that the client pick an option or two. Informed of the client's decision, the attorney again retreats to his law library and assembles a fully developed strategy, including a timeline and an estimate of which judge is likely to be assigned the case. (Some judges are more lenient than others; some judges are sloppier than others; some judges are too uncertain of their ground to treat your particular case carefully and thus may poorly address that case—and its client.) These procedures are well informed but individualized; they might be referred to as *controlled choice.*

To balance against this time-consuming process, the legal profession also has its special version of "influential" people, those who are known to be experts in a specific area of jurisprudence. Few laypeople challenge them on their special knowledge, which is unsurprising, likely due to the long history, complexity, and even mysteries of the field. Even looking into a law library can be inhibiting, with rows of similarly bound books and the labels on their spines.

Doctors are also faced with a multiplicity of choices on a given day. No doctor on the staff of a good hospital, for example, would dream of acting without consultation, save in a dire, life-threatening situation. The human body may be described in biology textbooks as if each one is similar to all the others, but doctors—and their patients—know better as they prepare plans for addressing different diseases. On the whole, we patients appreciate their expertise and their judgments. Only the most aggrieved of us challenge the diagnoses and remedies decided on by our physicians. It is important that they know us, but also that they know much more.

Dilemmas are also numerous in our profession. As someone with progressive political leanings, I'm a believer in choice, because, with all its complications and cautions, it is more likely to allow the student to be at the center of his own education. When he has a hand in choosing what he will learn and from whom he will learn it, there is a far greater chance that he will participate more freely and gladly, and that lies at the heart of learning.

Of course, adults do not and should not abdicate all authority over these matters. They provide the schools and hire the teachers; in most cases, teachers design the courses and offer them at specific hours in specific semesters. It is within a context of compromise that students make their way, though it is seen, and should be seen, more and more, as *their way*.

The first choice is that of which school to attend, and in that case, the important adults are the providers of the schools, and the parents who decide which school will best suit their child. For the rural parts of the nation, there may be only one school that is feasible, but in others there are different towns, or different schools within a town. The concept of choice is thus an old one in American education, albeit not usually identified as such. It is so familiar that we give it little notice.

Some may argue that we have a system that escapes totalitarianism, in that it gives families options. Private, parochial, and public charter schools exist to allow families to select among alternatives for schooling. The Francis W. Parker Charter Essential School, for example, offers a choice to the students of forty towns in central Massachusetts, some wealthy towns with well-provided middle and high schools, and others far less wealthy. Entry is by lottery, and except for siblings, each student has the same chance of being accepted as any other, as long as he and his family have attended an information session. Parker families do not need to have enough money for private school, nor do they have to live in the "right" public school district. The lottery is for us more than just a nice idea; it is an expression of some measure of freedom.

In the United States, parents usually exercise their choice of schools for their children by moving to a community where they feel that the public schools are likely to serve their children well, and if they have substantial or even moderate financial resources, they can make choices about where to live. In a suburb? In a community where there are both district schools and access to a "school of choice"—say, a high school of the arts or of the sciences—or a charter or pilot school that is small, making it likely that each child is known well and yet still has some class choices from which she can select? Or will the family choose to live in a community that shares their ethnicity and where they are comfortable with their neighbors, but in which the schools are not reputed to be successful? Underlying all these decisions is a job that is not too far away, and the availability of housing they can afford.

Families without alternatives—that is, families that do not have the resources or awareness of options to move to another district or to apply to a private or parochial school—send their children to whichever public schools are required to enroll them; these schools might be excellent or dull or, at worst, wasteful of the time of their teachers and students.

Put another way, all our public schools are, in fact, segregated, meaning that the chances are good that the school in which your child is enrolled is made up of classmates who look, speak, and act like him or her. These divisions are reinforced by class just as much as by race or ethnicity.

This segregation is not of the legal kind addressed by Martin Luther King Jr. and the civil rights movement. King wanted full and unqualified access to the public schools that were available to whites in the mid-1960s. That is, King wanted what the white folks had, with no alterations allowed, but because socioeconomic classifications determined the kinds of houses that everyone, whites or blacks, could afford, more than law would tend toward segregation. Class stratification often leads to racial segregation. And this is what has too often happened, in the North as well as the South.

During the 1960s and 1970s, faced with this situation, some urban-suburban regions created what were quickly termed "busing" arrangements, such as greater Boston's highly controversial student transportation scheme. This offered more racial and economic diversity to more children, but choice was restricted, and for that reason and others, many families responded by moving out of the district, thus resegregating.

Most private schools can offer admission only to those who are able to pay their fees, though the fees may vary. This restricts choice, though in many cases, a family may choose to live in a less desirable house or a less desirable area in order to have the money to pay for a private school. This offers the liberty and the market maneuverability that the public sector may not be able to provide.

Many private schools (that is, institutions that are licensed but not operated by public authorities) are schools of choice. The selection among them can be driven by religion ("I want a Jewish day school for my son and daughter") or by educational focus ("We are a traditional school where every student is enrolled in the 'basics' and is preparing for college") or by social justice ("We gather money privately to offer small classes and high standards to deserving youngsters" or "We are an 'international' school, picking children by lottery from within certain designated ethnic or racial groups"). This last category is small but growing, at least in Providence and Boston, two cities with which I am familiar.

The private schools with large endowments—which, not surprisingly, are old, allowing some of their graduates to have amassed substantial financial fortunes—have tapped the loyalties of their graduates who want to "give back." Some are like Phillips Academy in Andover, where I was headmaster for nine years in the 1970s; ironically, its wealthy status allowed it to enroll a wider socioeconomic and racial spread of students than were able to attend the local public high school.

A second form of choice occurs within the school that has been chosen. My most dramatic encounter with offering choice within a school was at Andover. We entrusted the scheduling task to a mathematics teacher who knew how to design and operate benign and efficient placement systems, and there was quiet acceptance that no one should hassle him or ask him for favors. "This school is impartial in its assignment to courses," we would say, and we got away with it. The risk was too high that I-the-headmaster might have to make a faculty complainer take the scheduling task, just to shut him up!

However, Andover also experimented with giving the students a more direct role in arranging each of their own course programs, and thereby, ultimately, the master schedule. This decision depended on our trust in students' judgments: *Who better than the teenager to know what is best at this moment in his or her schooling?* We called the process of student course selection "Arena Day," an odd choice of wording, as it brought forth images of ancient Roman fights to the death by two gladiators or a single gladiator and a vicious beast, such as a hungry lion. Exhibitions indeed!

At Andover's Arena Day, we teachers (I taught a seminar around our dining room table two terms out of three) sat at tables arranged in a large oval in the gymnasium. Instructors were grouped by department. We had signs in front of us, identifying the courses that we were offering. At a set moment, the gym doors were opened, and the students poured in, the seniors first, armed with the numbers that they had drawn in a lottery and a personal list arranged by subject and teacher, the most desired at the top. They, and only they, weighed their options: Would they get up early to take chemistry with the teacher who is reputed to be the clearest and most patient, or would they take the history elective that has interested them for years and meets at the same time? As course sections filled up, the more popular ones earlier, the remaining students had more limited options. The atmosphere, at first dominated by smoother and more experienced seniors, grew more raggedy for those who had never before had that particular kind of heartbreak. The process was also cruel to unpopular teachers. To this day I can recall the drawn face of one such person, a decent, well-informed scholar whose class was reputedly difficult—and early in the morning to boot.

Arena Day did not remain long. The scheduling officer, aided by computers, continued to observe the students' top three preferences but did his job in private. Technology specially designed for school scheduling did that task in a flash and brooked no complaints. Schedules were still determined by the students' own instincts as to what kind of teaching would suit them best. Moreover, three productive days were returned to the school's schedule.

"Why give kids and parents choices?" many skeptics ask, believing that these constituencies do not know enough to make decisions about the stuff of schooling, about when and how to proceed with each individual class. Further, giving adolescents choices is, some doubters say, like asking a baby who is still at the crawling stage to run a marathon. That attitude, all too common in some schools, still avoids the moral issue: *Who has the right to influence my child's mind? If I have such a right, what choices of schools or programs will the system make available?*

Who has that right indeed? This sort of issue is both paramount and rarely addressed in school systems that control, through state and district regulation and teachers' contracts with professional organizations, the shape of each school. Furthermore, when such battles are joined, they are more often described as a battle over a child's future than over the quality of his mind.

What would our world be like if we school people had almost total choice of what we wanted to do, with whom we wanted to do it, and the surety that no one else would object? What might the options be?

A school board and its superintendent would create within or across their district a variety of schools that, within state regulations, had diverse routes to a common, state-approved goal. They would balance the claims of every school's varied but relevant groups. Such schools would offer a menu of options from which parents and their offspring could select. Each of these options would be fully described on paper, and administrators and teachers would be on hand to advise, even cajole, families. The attitude of professional educators would be somewhat paternalistic: "We know what is best for your child even if we do not know her well," but would rarely be directly expressed.

Families, by means of a blind lottery, would make their choices, a list arranged in order of preference. The schools would be "filled" each autumn on the basis of the lottery. Exceptions would rarely be allowed, and those few would be largely for special needs students, as not all schools would be likely to offer all the required, mandated specialties, or for persons who live at great distances from some of the schools and who would often, for valid reasons, be late in the morning.

If I were admitted as a student in one of these schools, I could make a list of the teachers that I would like to have. Those teachers would have the choice to select me, but in a rotation so that certain teachers would not be able to take only the eager students—as often happens now in the tracking system. Finally, the state would have the choice of funding and endorsing any new or special program that was created on the basis of the wishes of a group of teachers and students. This process would be repeated at the end of each semester, save for yearlong courses that required stability.

Or I could choose to avoid any sort of organized, collective schooling and let other community offerings and my family alone forward my learning. There are some more radical, but interesting choices—alternatives to the high schools just described—to consider. For example, a public library could offer a program tilted toward the strongest parts of its collection, the most obvious being fiction and nonfiction writing. My teachers would be librarians to whom I could turn, if I wished, for counsel on which books to read. This library-based program could be on a course-by-course basis. For example, I might take my science and mathematics courses within a school and my English, foreign language, history, and government courses in the library. Internships in nearby businesses and laboratories might be relied on for extensive learning, as they are in the Met Schools all over the nation today, but also during the summer, by growing numbers of high school students.

How these alternatives to the school building would deal with teacher certification, school facilities laws, and mandatory testing would take some careful planning and perhaps charter or pilot school status. The idea for a public library–based school is not far-fetched; and the double use of public facilities could be cost saving as well as educationally powerful.

And then there is what is increasingly accepted as home-based schooling. This option is widely used today; there are associations of homeschoolers to advocate for this option and to provide assistance in launching such an effort. In a way, homeschooling can be considered an American right under the Constitution. Leaving my intellectual and social development up to me or my immediate relatives has logic of its own. We are animals, albeit animals with higher orders of intellectual acuity, and we should not be left alone to find our own understandings of our particular world.

The homeschooling option should be approached with caution, but it is not silly. We should be able to contemplate a mix of activities for our particular family and not just our school-age children. What special powers allow government to insist on its exact definition of what my child should have? History and civics should be there. Also economics, the means to assess this country's engines of wealth and sophistication about how to get from A to B. The trick for the state will be to inspect for quality and stability, just as it does—or should—for conventional schools.

• • •

In sum, choice is not a politically clever option to take certain parents—ones with easier offspring—away from mainstream schooling but, in the basic sense, a fundamental right in a democracy. Americans should not be in the habit of insisting on one best system, as the chances are that this one system will ram one set of facts, beliefs, and values down students' throats. Furthermore, what is considered the best way to learn for one student may be inappropriate for others.

Wise public authorities should support a flexible system of choices, with all its complications, and should find ways to make it less expensive. Such variety is an expression of responsible democracy.

CHAPTER · THIRTEEN

Faith

Education is an act of faith; and, curiously perhaps, that is why it is so important.

Paradoxically, compulsory institutional schooling is an abridgement of democratic freedom, yet it is also an understandable, necessary condition for that very freedom. Schools must value both individual inspiration and the harmony that can, in time and with considerable work, emerge from it.

Education is an invention, not a discovery. The need and the means for schooling were not just sitting there; we had to decide, whatever the naysayers might argue, that this is what we collectively needed. What the founders of America's first public schools thought arose from religious motives; they wanted to protect their children from what an early Puritan statement asserted was "that old deluder, Satan." Granted, seventeenth-century Boston was not a time and place that honored diversity; still, we have ever since held the belief that a few common values will be a protection for us all.

Although I have used the word "faith" to mean confidence in the truth and worth of others, thus willingness to temper one's individual desires to achieve a common good, faith as a word is also generally connected with organized religion. You can be asked "In what faith were you raised?" and in America these days your answer probably would be Catholic, Protestant, or Jewish; recently we would add Muslim, as we have come to acknowledge that Muslims also live in our midst and deserve recognition.

Most of us are chary of questioning the shape of, or the need for, a commitment to some spiritual being. American Unitarians straddle the gulf between belief in a distant, fixed being and a void. They say, "We are who we are; let us accept that, in the realization that there are no answers that all of us can find persuasive." At the same time, Unitarians believe that they will be understood as questing and spiritual people. They take this conviction on *faith*.

I was raised as a nonsectarian Protestant. With my family I attended Sunday services in Yale University's Battell Chapel, but I didn't go to Sunday school, where I might have learned more about the Bible or about other religions. Instead, I was dragged along to what for me were tedious occasions, which required uncomfortable clothes and being cautioned not to wiggle. I was given pads of paper on which I was expected to draw pictures silently. Was it this routine that was to stiffen my commitment to a Christian God? Still, from the beginning I liked the music.

At Pomfret School, I attended weekday and Sunday services, with only Saturday providing a break. Back at Yale as an undergraduate student, I sang in the Battell choir and served as a chaplain's assistant, passing the donation plate across rows of worshippers, and, as the plate filled up, trying hard to keep the dollar bills from floating to the floor. The Army took me to Germany, but I found the military chaplains far too fundamentalist for my taste; I took a vacation from organized religion. Nancy and I tried our hand at teaching Sunday school in the local Unitarian Church during our first year of marriage, but later at Harvard, I attended few services at the university's Memorial Church, finding them stifling, singsong, and full of "assurances" that struck me as having no place in a research university. Of course, it was also true that our children were small in those years, and I welcomed Sunday mornings as a time when I could be with them.

The headmaster's schedule at Phillips Academy included dutiful attendance at Christian services; the requirement for students had only recently been lifted at the insistence of the school minister, who preferred fewer sincere worshippers to many reluctant ones. A few years later, when he died and in recognition of our varied population, we decided to offer Protestant, Catholic, and Jewish services (the first two in the school chapel and the third at a local synagogue), and to do that we hired a minister, a priest, and a rabbi who taught English and history classes and offered varied spiritual experiences as well as services. Numbers continued to be small at the Sunday services, but our three "street priests" were popular and influential all over the school—and throughout the week. Nancy and I enjoyed regular attendance for the whole time we were there, and saw it as much more than a duty; we learned as much about our own faith as about those of others. And, of course, as a former Phillips graduate and cartoonist Jeff McNelly has said, "As long as there are history tests, there will always be prayer in schools."

Today, retired and living in the country during the academic year, we listen to the services at Harvard University Memorial Church—thanks to Harvard's student-run radio station, WHRB—from comfortable chairs in our home, looking out of its wide windows to the deep forests and mountain to the west, these changing shape and color depending on the season. For my whole life I have been moved by church music, and the music in these services is superb. My earlier reservations about liturgy and Bible stories in a modern university have been laid to rest. The preacher of the university is the Baptist Peter Gomes; his words are as poetic as they are provocative. I have come to take notes on these occasions, jottings that have influenced several of the observations in this book.

Organized traditional religion has a long history, and its current proponents need make no apology for it. It appears to serve some people well, albeit a shrinking number as a percentage of the national population. Religion in our tradition remains a private matter. What I believe is something that I can keep to myself; it is no one else's business. Some hucksters gather the timid faithful and give them hope by means of colorful preaching and singing in enormous church auditoriums; some of the money gathered there ends up in the preachers' pockets. These people sell faith, and there is no serious sin in that as long as there are willing buyers. Among all sorts of products, religion is one of the safest; few adults are harmed. Children, though, are another matter, as they are likely to believe literally all that they hear. The lucky ones are those who have parents who talk with them and help them sort out what they believe from what they have heard.

Very few schools have their own church services, but many wrestle with the problem of whether to teach religion in their academic classes. This is not surprising. The word, and its accepted substance, carries universally important freight. The formal religions drive many of the major controversies of our time. For example, in many ways what has come to be called the Iraq War is a struggle among Muslims—Sunnis and Shias—and also between Muslims and English-speaking Christians. Next door to this conflict is the seemingly endless strife between Jews and Muslims in Israel. Still further away are the hundreds of years of bitter differences between Catholics and Protestants in Ireland. An understanding of the roots and natures of these conflicts, complicated and ever moving though they are, is essential in order to move beyond gathering static myths. Most older students find this an engaging inquiry and would like to study it in school.

The formal study of history also requires an understanding of the influence of religion. One cannot appreciate the extraordinary international influence of Mohandas Gandhi without taking into account his spiritualism. Like Jesus in a way, he did not say, "Do this"; rather he said, "Follow me." Religion is a trek, not a code that one can define and then repeat like some sort of prayer of remorse—or praise.

One cannot understand contemporary American politics without attending to the dictates of formal Protestant religions, as has been apparent in the long reign in the White House of members of the Bush family. Bill and Hillary Clinton showed and still show the same proclivity to look to the Bible for guidance. Mike Huckabee, a candidate for the Republicans in the 2008 presidential election, was an ordained minister; his religiosity appeared to be an asset, not a liability.

Religion does not fit into a neat academic category. Its influence is both cultural and political. In the past, for example, the preacher Norman Vincent Peale had striking influence. Why? Could such a powerful figure exist in our Internet-driven era? The list of questions is endless.

America is hardly a secular nation. The way it spends its time and money, the issues it allows to dominate its public discussion, are testaments to that complicated truth. High school students and teachers have to understand that, and not sweep that critical subject under some convenient table.

Public high schools have a two-sided task here. Religion is part of our past, part of all our histories without exception, as mankind has long had to struggle to find an answer to the unknowable. Teachers have hesitated to put religion into the curriculum, however, partly because of the practical, political realities arising from the separation of church and state, and the danger that speaking about such private matters in a public forum may well lead to proselytizing. The Bible can be said to be a form of excessively focused "truths," as can the Koran. Many devoted worshippers accept the statements in these documents as received truth, these texts encapsulating what they believe is revealed wisdom, not just the wisdom of ancient peoples but of a deity, even of a creator.

Most modern theologians, however, believe that the ancient texts give us general directions, not precise guides for action, guideposts rather than hitching posts. Those scholars who claim that some aspects of ancient dogma are truth (some of which may defy precise translation into modern language and thus conduct) should be considered as dangerous as they are arrogant.

Adolescents have to understand the difference between these two postures, a task that they often find frustrating in its lack of sharp edges and, many of them believe, in its irrelevance to their lives. Indeed, living with religion in a democracy is an issue that bedevils the U.S. Supreme Court. Yet it must be addressed.

Most public educators dodge these issues as if they would cause a plague. However, the Francis W. Parker Charter Essential School, I am proud to say, builds the world's religions into its core curriculum. The intent there is informative, on the assumption that one cannot understand the human past without pondering our predecessors' acceptance of the world's "deliberate unknown." It is part of life and cannot and should not be kept away from students' school experience and analysis.

Are we Americans hypocrites? No, that charge is too strong. Understandably, mixed feelings are part of any individual person's identity. Well, then, are we propounding that morality and religion are the same thing? Is a set of church-assigned virtues inevitably moral? Are we implying that the prospect of being irreligious is unimaginable? Perhaps the normal human process of growing up is disappearing, as Edgar Z. Friedenberg insisted in his book *The Vanishing Adolescent* some years ago. If he is right, how do we in our New American High School help our adolescents find their own answers to the questions they are facing?

The world is full of mystery. No one of us can explain why it is that human beings exist on this earth. No one of us can say for sure just why the sun rises over the eastern hills at a predictable time. We claim that records collected over decades increase our knowledge and predict patterns, yet we know, deep down, that all that might change. We keep that worry, that wonder, that gratitude very deep; they provide a starting place, an anchor, but one that, we know, can be dragged in a big storm or a shift in the sands below. All these thoughts and feelings influence, in one way or another, the way that we keep school.

CHAPTER · FOURTEEN

Morality

Religion may be connected to morality, but it is only part of the moral issue in schooling. The broader mission is to help students become more responsible and thoughtful. To do that, we must not only give students practice but offer helpful feedback. The judicious person is one who is not dependent on others yet who knows whom to consult in confusing and trying times; the decision is finally hers, but she nevertheless does the right thing, meaning the thing that will help more than harm in the short but also the long run. Morality is a universal set of beliefs that is meant to help those who are facing these kinds of dilemmas; acting on these principles is a habit, one that school personnel carefully reinforce. Teachers must make clear that there is a fine—but inevitably fuzzy—line between guidance and control, for the simple reason that control doesn't last, and guidance often does. We may influence our students, but they will live the bulk of their lives away from us.

Teaching is a moral act, as it involves an older person or persons who have authority—that is, legitimate power—over younger persons. This imposed authority will not be a surprise to anybody. On the whole, older people know more than younger people; they are often expected to take care of them; and it is a clear duty that these elders pass along the best of their inherited wisdom to their juniors.

In most cultures, acceptable thought and conduct (morality) is culturally defined: "This is what 'goes' here, and this is what does 'not go.'" Most cultures are coherent, but there are, alas, places in this world that are without accepted order; they are lawless, with power in the hands only of those who can marshal it. Cynicism and despair are more likely to be inherited in such venues, to the detriment of their children.

Because of these cultural differences, the formal teaching of the need for order—and, not only that, but of the need for justice in whichever "order" is currently in force in a community—is a task packed with dangers, the greatest being that the older folks, as part of their moral agenda, will load onto the minds of the younger people ideas and opinions that do not particularly deepen their understanding of the world, but instead steer the young minds into a direction that the older people desire. That danger is palpable today, with federal, state, and local governments loading their schools' required curricula and tests to ensure that knowledge, however temporary, has settled firmly in each adolescent's or child's head. The bias of the government's priorities is transparent, but nevertheless, as a political matter, asserted. Progress for these reformers is considered social justice in the form of acceptance of uniform standards. They want the best for everyone, but without offering each child the ultimate respect of being seen as a separate person, with separate needs and separate definitions of what "the best" is.

Thus Americans' reserve about the appropriateness of any policies of the currently elected leadership is justified. No one group, in power or not, is likely to have everything right, and times change; what made sense yesterday may not make sense today. While we Americans must be respectful of government, we must at the same time insist on the right to disagree and to work to change policy. Our students must recognize the advantage of diversity, even rifts, in our nation's values. Democracy is stronger for its clash of demands on its citizens and for the time it takes to compromise these differing viewpoints.

I have seen too many examples of times when schools avoided time-consuming but crucial conversations about social justice, individual freedom and responsibility, even the meaning of life. These ponderings are recognizable in religion, in the formal religion of churches and synagogues, the middle-of-the-night questionings of adults, and the naive daydreaming of children. Of course, young ones may not be as naive as we might assume. Why, they may ask, is Daddy off in Afghanistan risking his life and taking those of others? Isn't that unfair? Susie's dad is here at home: Why can't mine be? Why should my dad be scared all the time; isn't he scared with all the shooting going on around him? You always tell me to be careful. Is he being careful?

Parents know that the children deserve good answers from the people who mean the most to them, and teachers are often among those people. Presumably, Daddy is risking his life and threatening that of others in order to create the peaceful and openhearted community that we all, when we think carefully about it, desire. The child presses on: Why can't someone besides Daddy help those who are being attacked? Neither parent nor teacher should dodge these good questions with bromides or a dismissive "I don't know." Wonderings don't go away; they affect the quality of classrooms—and childhoods.

High school students need to engage in and learn from these "reconnaissances"—going over familiar ground in order to recognize the old but also to get a new perspective on it—in both the intellectual as well as the physical dimensions. Give them a question or complex situation: "What do you make of this? Explain what you determine to me and bounce the matter off some classmates." Then review the matter in class, sorting out the steps that each person or team of students took in order to come up with an agreement. Were those the only compromises that made sense? Or were there better ones? If so, how do you analyze and defend them?

I understand that all such ponderings of global priorities are so demanding that they can become wearisome and, at their worst, freighted with self-righteousness. However, I believe that in a world in which information can be gained by individuals on their own, schools exist to be the common areas in which such discussions can be held. Slowly and subtly, some common purposes can be acknowledged, and our responsibilities as citizens can be acknowledged. If schools exist only to allow certain students to establish advantage over others, that point is lost.

There are deep costs in shunting moral concerns aside. One cost is a government that focuses only on how to protect the flanks that it believes are important. Another is an environment in which the words of leaders like Gandhi and Martin Luther King have been lost.

There have, of course, also been moments in which the nation was threatened, such as the attack on Pearl Harbor and the decision of the Congress to declare war, to force individual citizens to do what they might not have chosen to do, and to mobilize not only the citizens but also industry. I believe that these decisions, however difficult and costly, were, at core, not only practical but also moral ones. Fascism was inconsistent with democracy; and if we believed in democracy and believed that our democratic system was in grave danger, we had to fight in its defense. In the name of the war effort, however, the government treated its Japanese American citizens harshly and without attention to their legitimate rights to property and liberty. Thus the making of moral judgments is tricky; it can become arrogant. When decisions have to be taken, they must be carried through with extraordinary restraint.

Today a parent may legitimately ask, "Who has the authority to mess with my child's mind?" Who indeed, and by what right? The question is an apt one. The original responsibility is clearly the parents' to mess with—or to help develop—their child's mind. Those who want to help the parents in this important endeavor must do so sensitively. They must avoid overreaching even when their intent is to direct youth toward a goal of peace.

Parents—and the teachers who help them, working directly with their children—may well ask, "Does the 'state' [defined both as our formally elected representatives and those groups that are nonelected, albeit usually well-intentioned, nongovernmental groups] have a right to influence our child? Do the private sector and its well-financed advertising industry have such a right? Are hot sales the measure of goodness, or merely of success? Do our common values still exist? Or have they been shattered by the hammers of the culture, a surrender to the perceived need for endless competition, the influence of the market economy, and its incessant and intrusive commercialism?"

What is the teachers' role in protecting their students? Are we educators satisfied that the gathering, analysis, and use of a set of test scores to drive policy and practice are needed and wholly proper in a free society? Does frequent standardized assessment help us teach better? Or do those scores, and the system they represent, remove the individuality that otherwise emerges, from birth onward, with genuine intellectual development? Can these two different goals be reconciled? Can they exist side by side?

Just as the parents set the tone inside a child's home, teachers have a special responsibility for the moral lessons and atmosphere that will permeate the school: the child's first community. It takes a village to raise a child, the sensible truism asserts. What are the boundaries of a community? A single classroom? A grade level? A school? A neighborhood? And just who are *we* who are raising this child? Everyone in the nation? In a state? In a city or town? In an extended family?

Is the role of a school merely to provide guidance for each child's learning activities, as a widely used, jargon-filled textbook intones? Is that process limited to crap detecting, raking the worthy from the unworthy as it already exists, but not leaving time for the child to develop his own contribution?

Should our schools focus their energies on the child's likely future? Does this also mean the expected future of the place where the students in a particular community live? Or the expected future for a region or a state or this country or the world writ large? The answers to this question may well determine what kind of curriculum is needed, but they may also endanger the future of the child who, for one reason or another, decides to live elsewhere as an adult.

These are good and reasonable concerns, ones that we must take seriously in our New American High School. Many educators working close to children, alas, repress them. We know that narrow biases are embedded in many schools and that raising questions about them is clearly apt, but all too often we put them out of their minds. "Come on," we say or think, "we cannot be the referees of everything that goes on here. We are not jailers, or at least we don't mean to be. We can't help it if they don't like learning math."

• • •

There's a fight in the schoolyard. On the first snowy day of the year, most of the students enjoy some mild roughhousing, but now a group of kids is attacking some others with hard, icy snowballs. Some teachers observe the melee. Should they ignore it, or should they intervene before someone gets hurt?

In the cafeteria, one table full of kids starts putting down the group at a nearby table. "You guys are a bunch of fags," they churlishly mutter. Some teachers hear the slur. If they do not decisively and clearly intervene, the interpretation among some students will be that such name-calling is OK. They may even believe that some teachers agree that a kid is a "fag," whatever that epithet might mean in that setting.

An overweight child is joked about, often within his or her hearing. Some of the jeerers may delight in the heavy kid's embarrassment. They pay no attention to what he or she might feel. A clumsy kid may try out for a varsity sport for each of the three seasons and get chosen for none. "You really are a clod!" A pregnant teacher may be the object of ridicule. "She must be giving birth to an elephant!" A bus driver may be the butt of jokes even as he or she is driving. Kids may open windows and shout to people on the sidewalks, "Help! We're being driven by a blind man!"

These examples will be familiar to many teachers. Only people who work out of the earshot of students (and some thoughtless teachers) will find them bizarre: "Oh no. Our children don't do that. That behavior may be seen in *other* schools, but not *ours*. Our kids are *good* kids."

What is deliberately hurtful? What is insensitive? What is "only kidding," even affectionate? Each example requires its own history, its own analysis. Who knows what's really going on, and therefore what we should do? It is confusing and dangerous in the sense that children can be hurt, and no serious school can simply ignore these issues. Schools should be moral communities that aim for relations between both adults and children who are behaving well. The street corner doesn't aim for such a culture, but schools are definitely not street corners. Perhaps a faculty member cannot intervene on every occasion, but the students must know that the adults will not stand for behavior that offends and therefore harms.

Our large, anonymous high schools make things worse here. It is hard to protest examples of bad behavior in a school in which students have the impression that each of them is known by only a few of the adults and cared about by even fewer of them, and that the assistant principals are often the school's only police. Thereby the moral issue provides another strong argument for small schools or small, enclosed units within a large school, in which any adult—and even some of the students—can address issues of moral concern and build a tone of consistent respect.

• • •

Moral concerns on the part of educators have a long history. Back in the seventeenth century, school people expressed what they termed a "fear of barbarism" that so terrified educators that they saw their roles as "civilizing the savages"—that is, the children. These days, however, we educators are too often embarrassed to put moral issues on our faculty meeting agendas. Sometimes we feel that we might not know the religious and moral convictions of even those colleagues with whom we are most familiar. At other times, we know what our beliefs—and our differences—are, but we are uncertain as to how to discuss them.

At the same time, we also know that we should not avoid these sticky matters. Issues of morality and principled behavior must be at the center of a school's work. To dismiss the implications of this reality with the statement that "schools are secular" and that as a result we have no authority to teach (much less preach) the roots of principled action and behavior is a weak excuse.

This tradition of "secular morality" goes far back in our history, nearly as far as the fear of barbarism. Although most of the early settlers on our shores may have come for the right to practice a religion as they saw fit, a right denied them in Europe, the issue of how these religious groups might happily coexist arose almost immediately. We set to work to find such common ground as we could. We have the First Amendment to the Constitution, but we also have coins which tell us that "In God We Trust." At presidential swearing-in ceremonies, a chaplain is present and says a prayer calling for divine guidance for the nation's new leader as well as for the people writ large. In these ceremonies, mixed signals abound. Still, one way a new leader can address moral obligations, including those that are humbler than those expressed at presidential inaugurations, is by being clear on likely results: on where he or she wants to head and why, and what the most likely options are for getting there.

• • •

So, what to do in our new school? We and our students must understand our history and at the same time bear witness to a high standard of moral behavior that connects well with current needs. We must be familiar with examples so that we can examine their moral dimensions. One 1960s-era "bearing of witness" for me was the Peace Corps; the name of the program was clear and instructive. I was involved in the training of one of the first groups of passionate young volunteers; my job was to brief them on how American high schools were designed and meant to function—as though the high schools in the economically distressed communities where they were likely to be working would be quite like ours. Because so many aspects of our work were different, I concentrated on the purposes of high schools and what they were supposed to add to a young person's life. I was the blind teacher leading blind students, but I was the best, apparently, that Harvard authorities could roll out for the edification of these principled and brave young men and women.

Another example from my personal experience arises from a large—and, alas, naive—human resource development project that the Harvard Graduate School of Education (HGSE) undertook in the western region of Nigeria a few years later. Funded by the U.S. government (indeed, suggested by its African USAID regional staff), it involved the design and early operation of a high school shaped along the lines of an American secondary school. It was called Aiyetoro, after the little village nearby. Edward Kaelber, who had been an associate dean at the HGSE, was appointed to be its principal for the first few years. The Nigerians had no role in his appointment; the courtesy did not occur to us or to the federal staff members urging the project on us. In hindsight, that omission is embarrassing. Even more extraordinary, Ed had never been a high school principal; his expertise was in finance and administration. Ed's wife came with him as an important member of the team, thereby indicating by her presence that women are and can be part of a venturesome bureaucracy.

This seemed like useful and polite symbolism to us, but we weren't sure what the Nigerians made of it.

Despite the disorderly start, Ed's manner greatly helped the situation; his down-to-earth Maine background served him—and the Nigerians—well. He readily admitted that he was unsure about certain details or uncertain about their effectiveness. The project did move forward, the jungle was cleared, the building was erected, the staff was hired and set about its work, and the transition to Nigerian control came on schedule, in a warm and friendly manner, as far as we could tell. The work was professional in all respects.

Later during the same decade, the State Department asked me to go to Nigeria on two basic missions: to advise the regional governments on what their high schools might become—a task made complex because each region reflected the religious and tribal convictions of its populace, such as the communities of Yorubas and Hausas—and to explain why and how our system has evolved. Of course, this attempt to help, like the earlier ones, was somewhat of a stab in the dark.

One day while driving in our American-hired air-conditioned multiseat van on the way to visit Aiyetoro, we passed a young white man who was walking with a large but clearly empty sack on his shoulder. As he heard us coming, he turned and flagged us down. Could we give him a lift, he asked, toward the west? He had heard that there was an American-supplied new high school there; he hoped to be able to talk its managers into giving him some paper, pens, grease pencils, and such for him to carry back to his school. We assured him that the rumors about the school were true and urged him to pile into the car with us. He jumped in and promptly fell asleep. When we arrived, he told us that he was a Peace Corps volunteer. While his clothes were in a washing machine, he took a long, hot shower, then joined us at the dinner table, regaling us with fascinating stories of his school. After a few more days of well-deserved R&R, he let us drive him back to his school, laden with equipment. I felt as if I should have paid him tuition.

This young person would probably joke if he heard us label him a particularly moral man. I guess that he would say that he was off on an adventure, or just doing his duty, paying back for being an economically favored and politically free American citizen. His attitude then is mirrored today by the decision of many young American men and women who join the Peace Corps and similar groups, but also the armed services. They may feel that the cause for which they are working is wise and timely, a way to help.

We had an additional experience in Nigeria that made an equally great impression on me. Driving at the usual hair-raising high speed so favored by our skilled Nigerian driver, we came abruptly upon a serious automobile wreck, the scattered pieces smoldering and the dust still flying. Seemingly from nowhere in the bush rushed a group of Nigerian women, who picked up a baby who had been thrown from the car and started to clean him off, cuddling and cooing to him. Some men put out the car's flames and pushed it as upright as was possible. All these people were working at great personal risk, as the car could have exploded. They exemplified a moral commitment of great courage.

Not all examples of generosity and courage come from abroad. Most of us Americans are favored people, though we are loath, even embarrassed, to admit it. Among us still are those who volunteer to help others in both consistent and spontaneous ways. Our small mid-Massachusetts town's fire department has been, until recently, largely made up of volunteers. The men and women there agree to extensive training on their own time by the state fire marshal's staff, followed by annual "brush-ups" to keep their skills and their familiarity with new equipment current. They take part in the town's big annual event—the Independence Day parade—and ride slowly along the route with sirens blaring, throwing small candies to the children in the crowd. The emergency medical technicians in our town—our "911"—are also volunteers, and until recently their services were free. I personally was the beneficiary of their expertise after I fell down in our bedroom and was unable to get up due to the weakening effects of cancer. The rescue crew arrived within minutes, whisked me to the hospital emergency room, and stood by until they saw that I was in good hands. That one of these workers was also the person who sold us our computer and saw to its regular maintenance made this very personal for me. He, however, as is his wont, made a joke: "Ted! We have to stop meeting like this! Isn't it enough that I fix your computer?"

When high school students do volunteer work on these EMT rescue crews, it is time well spent. There is reciprocity here. What is good for the recipients of care is also good for the students who provide the care. For many, it is the first time in their lives that they see people in need of things and services that they may take for granted; they realize that most of them have never experienced genuine neediness. They also realize that they are old enough, and skilled enough, to offer real help.

Other kinds of activities are closer to home, built around asking the older students to give blood to those who are sick, or to fast (or, my favorite, to eat gruel) for a meal and give the money saved to hunger relief, or to refrain from speaking for a day in order to support those who have been "silenced" by the mores in our society. These are short-term sacrifices, but especially if they are done with others, they can have long-term effects, at least on the donors. When I was at Phillips Academy in Andover in the 1970s, our excellent tripartite ministry (a minister, priest, and rabbi) as well as other teachers sponsored a number of these kinds of initiatives. The voluntary gatherings were without sermons, but when the donors described, among much laughter and teasing, the sense of purpose that these activities awoke in them, they were very moving.

Without being preachy and holier than thou, we need to make more of these empathic and generous instincts. We could precede each academic year with a couple of days of orientation to our school community, organized primarily by older student volunteers. The faculty must take care that these volunteers are not just what their peers perceive as "goody-goody" types; the student orientation teams must represent a fair spectrum of the older students. Faculty and parent representatives should also be involved. In recent years at Phillips Academy in September, alumni also join in "Non-Sibi [Not for Oneself—the school's motto] Day" in many areas of the country and even the world. There might be some short, apt essays that are used to give initial focus to the discussion groups that follow the work.

For some adolescents, it's random acts of kindness, chosen by themselves, that seem preferable to group projects. Inevitably, some sharp and usually sincere students will raise the issue of their independence. "Must we be all alike?" they will ask. "Should we be all alike?" "Is it proper for a school—and the government that directs it—to hammer us into one sort of person?" "Where is the room for dissent?" "Is dissent a good thing?"

Teachers must be sensitive to this sort of reaction, both when it is heard and when it appears to be absent. A project that seems to require uniformity will send a signal to some of the students, surely, that there is one and only one desired conduct tolerated in this shared space. Democracy itself is, at its best, governed by shared core beliefs, convictions that guide the progress of affairs. Some students may have seen this in the way that the nation, its states, and communities like their own nominate their potential leaders. Most nominating forums are tense and noisy places, but the best of them gather together when the final votes of the delegates have been passed. The students should start learning about that.

Critics may cavil at this. Isn't independence what we should be teaching? they may ask. Isn't that sort of independence a prime American value? Each citizen is to be valued for his or her opinion. That opinion can and should be challenged if it appears to rest on fallacious thinking or wrong facts, but the tenor of the exchanges must remain civil. My colleague at Harvard, Daniel Patrick Moynihan, later a senator from New York, famously said, "You're entitled to your own opinion, but you're not entitled to your own facts." Understanding both of these dimensions is essential to civil discussion and to democracy. In practice, this is difficult to monitor in a school—or anywhere else. One person's reasonable judgment of what is civil may not be another's, but the conversation itself will be enlightening.

• • •

Another useful word to shape how we deal with moral matters is *harmony.* That is, we want harmonious schools, defined as "having components elements pleasingly and appropriately combined." Yet another word is *delight,* meaning "taking pleasure and joy." The staff and students at such schools would value the "crafting" of joy. How? Celebrate staff and student birthdays. Find ways to honor the arrival of a staff member's baby or the other children in the newborn's family, perhaps with student-made "presents" of one sort and another, depending on the students' relationship with the new parents.

Schools should also quickly face up to an issue that is "disharmonious," perhaps calling a school meeting to address it. This may be more easily and quickly addressed in a small school where most everyone knows everyone else. In a large school, groups could meet by homerooms or, if the school had been broken up into smaller units—clusters of students and staff—in those units. Larger meetings can be informative and even inspirational as the school together confronts a schoolwide problem; but only in a smaller group can a student have the chance to voice her own reactions. When we at the Francis W. Parker Charter Essential School came together again after the Columbine tragedy ten years ago, we offered our students both venues: a large meeting and then one in each advisory. The language in each was starkly different: the larger one was respectful but quiet, and was dominated by adults; the smaller one was age-appropriate and emotional, and reflected how well each student felt known by his or her peers.

• • •

So, what does all this have to do with a New American High School and moral issues? A great deal. How to teach toward it? Several examples:

First, instruct the youngsters about the virtues and vices of "advertising." Attracting public attention is a worthy goal in many situations, especially in the functioning of a capitalist democracy. Students could write "ads" to be used in the "real world," ideally for a local candidate for public office; they could follow up with the candidate's campaign to see how that pitch is doing. Or the issue could be kept at home; an individual or team could prepare a speech on a topic in which there was clear interest in the school (such as tightening fire safety procedures) and deliver it at an assembly. If two (or more) students are on opposite sides of such an issue, stage a debate that is followed by a vote on the topic (not on the speakers' delivery or style).

A second example: each student could select and analyze some advertisements or articles that had been written and published to bend the reader's support. Did the authors cross a line between reasonable truth and deliberate misrepresentation?

A third: a group of students could prepare an "ad campaign" around a serious, relevant issue in their school (for example, an issue in front of their board of education of whether to renovate an existing building or to build a new one from scratch). Or a student could sign on to a local candidate's campaign for office and prepare an analysis for the class—and the candidate—to assess in hindsight.

If we believe in the necessity of all of us in a democracy to engage in a principled but relentless effort to pursue the truth—wherever that search may take us—the schools must systematically teach toward that goal and protect that teaching and learning from those with narrow, partisan, or theological complaints. The schools' central goal of teaching the principled use of the mind requires serious focus in the core curriculum.

This is a major role for every New American High School.

It is an old goal. The following dicta were found on a tablet in Old Saint Paul's Church in Baltimore, Maryland, dated 1692:

Be on good terms with all persons.

Enjoy your achievements as your plans.

Exercise caution in your business affairs; for the world is full of trickery.

Be yourself. Especially do not feign affection.

Be careful. Strive to be happy.

As you are designing a high school that will allow for these kinds of activities, don't be too quick to accept teachers' consternation about where your plan may be leading. Help them become part of these wider discussions. Understand their worry and impatience, but do not give in to it.

Be polite, but firm. Be flexible; use what is already in place; beware of new fads that may be around—a flashy op-ed in a local newspaper, for example, that appears to mock you and that is likely to be read by many, even most, of your constituents. Address the issue where the facts are untrue or the bias is evident; at least these critics are paying attention to you, thereby provoking interest in your work on the part of additional citizens. Criticism can be a political boon if you have thought things through so carefully that you are ready for it.

Moral behavior—moral awareness and duty—has a long, worthy history in America. That history must have an honored place, especially—as now—at a time of war and a deeply divided and suspicious polity. The risks for us teachers are substantial as we tell our students, "This is what happened, and this is what it means." At heart, however, teaching is the bearing of witness, acknowledging that this is what I, and ultimately you, must do.

CHAPTER · FIFTEEN

The Prospect

The prospect is bright. The American people—at least those paying attention—are restlessly, vocally waiting for a major new direction in education.

Many of us know that ours is a "democracy at risk," as in the widely read 1983 report from Washington, *A Nation at Risk.* "Reform" will come slowly, but it will come—as long as we organize ourselves to press for it.

The case for change is relatively easy to make, as there is a mountain of evidence available that demonstrates the ineffectiveness of our century-old practices. No frontal protest to what we have advocated can be challenged on the basis of facts now at hand. The research is there. Already there are new (or redesigned "old") schools that bear witness to the fact that the people and the polity are ready for a basic rethinking of how and why and what our children must learn. There are charter and in-district pilot schools to visit. There are large school systems moving to change what they do and how they do it, from New York City to Los Angeles to Denver. These efforts wax and wane as leaders and public sentiments come and go, but the roots of truly "new" American high schools are deeply set.

Yet there must be strong and sustained advocacy and political protection for these schools. The arguments in their favor may over time use differing rhetoric, but the substance will remain. Clusters of schools and states may gather themselves for mutual benefit and the exchange of evidence of the effectiveness or ineffectiveness of their emerging practices. The Coalition of Essential Schools, the KIPP schools, and comparable initiatives are widely seen across the country.

The private sector—foundations and businesses—have been and must continue to be engaged, and for the long haul. The example of the Gates and Carnegie Foundations are prime examples here; their leaders have been a step ahead of the establishment professionals for several decades.

Independent study and research efforts are necessary, but we also need vehicles for spreading what the scholars have learned—and are learning. The journal *Education Week*, for example, has supplied consistently accurate, interesting, and fair-minded reporting. Newspapers must have full-time education columnists on their staffs, a tradition started most effectively at the *New York Times*. Public television has helped, but must take this on as a major priority.

Ultimately most important, but still in flux, are the schools of education; they need the evidence-based authority now enjoyed by faculties of law, business, and (at some universities) public administration. Too many of these schools today are too often merely the bases for professors' personal consulting businesses. The best of these are useful, but too many are reduced to slides on an overhead projector: "Here are the Seven Steps to Educational Success"—success based on tests designed by the professor and administered by him or her.

There will be, in time, many truly "new" American high schools. There is demand for them, and the recent successes in many communities of focused pilot and charter schools and systemwide "decentralization" suggest that the political time is at hand for a new beginning, on a scale comparable in importance with the great movements of the late nineteenth century and the first decades of the twentieth.

Where there are children, there will be schools. The "sorts" of schools will vary, from the well organized to the catch-as-catch-can, all part of a state-mandated "system" such as that provided most Americans. Wars will intervene. Families will flee from creditors or natural disasters or toward a new, attractive job; and many will be on the move just to find communities more to their liking. Americans have been restless since their earliest days,

Our questions are not "Shall we have places for learning that will and must serve every child to the age of eighteen?" "Shall we finance them by a system of universal taxation, as this is a basic American right?"

We appear to have answered those two questions in the affirmative. The next questions then are "What should these places be like?" "What should they teach?" "Who should staff them?" "Can an imaginative teaching force be gathered for this purpose, and will the communities that hire them persist in providing the conditions of work and salary adjustments that are required?" "What should the penalties be for those who ignore their duty to send their children off for an education or who refuse to support school taxes because they have no children currently of school age?"

Although all these questions are obvious to many thoughtful Americans of our generation, the fact is that we are not acting on them and doing all that we should for many students, especially the neediest among them. We are yet not sensitive to the need for an environment that focuses on children, that attracts and holds a core of the best teachers around whom a strong, new American High School can flourish, a place that the children deserve.

Happily, the buildings that we need are there in most places, as are the other appurtenances of schools—playing fields, parking lots, covered hockey rinks, libraries, laboratories. They must be kept up and replaced, but what goes on inside them is the more challenging problem. Some students will always appear to be "unteachable," their minds and bodies obeying other masters, absorbed in interests that cannot be met in high schools as we currently operate them. Imagination and persistence (and political support) will help find ways to create approaches that serve these varied teenaged populations.

There will never be One Best way for all young people to learn the basic skills and understandings that our democratic society requires. The main fallacy in the argument that we should have One Best system (with One Best curriculum and One Best test and One Best kind of teacher) is that each of us, squeezing into a restricted system, will have to give up too much of what we really know how and want to do. Too many already just "Do School," in Denise Pope's words, with little sense that what they are learning will ever help them. This leads to the passivity and even cynicism that cause so many problems today. Governments need to understand that although they can help, they must not dictate. It is the genius of every community in every time that must be consulted and respected. As Deborah Meier says, "The most powerful people in a child's education should be those who know him or her." Only in this way will students, their families, and their teachers be properly served. Teachers need a variety of opportunities, each designed to serve a particular purpose and population. The colleges and the media must be drawn into this work; their substantive strength and political influence are necessary as we provide differentiation without the stigma of hierarchy. If we come together in such a movement, we will affirm our common humanity, and even the less religious among us will say, "This is the Lord's work."

As long as those of us who are convinced that a new kind of American high school is required are at once patient and resilient, the future appears bright. Pressure will increase, and arguments about the serious flaws in the way that we provide formal, mandatory education to adolescents will become widespread. A growing public awareness and impatience will spur fresh thinking and, ultimately, decisive action within government. Pressure from an informed media will keep the process moving.

The key participants will be—must be—local, state, and federal lawmakers and the media. Schools of education that lever the courage and incentives for their universities' leaders will be crucial; without the so often mocked education establishment's being fully engaged, change will not happen.

Some critics will quickly dismiss this strategy, asserting sneeringly that the so-called ed schools are too weak and too strangled in their jargon to act freely and imaginatively. Fiddling with the safe, surface issues in reform and acting as though scores of papers delivered at professional meetings constitute real progress are inadequate, even insulting. "Tinkering" will not do the trick.

I grieve about this, as I am an "educationist" myself and have been the dean of a graduate school of education. That I have seen our trade from the inside makes my impatience informed and plausible. The universities *can* do far better and will, if the pressure on them is sustained and well documented.

If the New American High Schools are to meet their original intentions, they must grow in number and in related influence. Only a critical mass of schools—perhaps several hundred spread across a dozen states—will withstand some government's wish to smother them for their "crime" of not following precise, top-down direction from the authorities in power. Private citizens must know about their schools and, where necessary, organize to protect them. They must honor and promote the more progressive and engaging aspects even in traditional schools. There is a necessary politics to school reform, and reformers must not shirk it.

Political action groups must relentlessly press for reform. The schools deserve as much ink as the sports and fashion departments of typical papers; the periodic essay or column or an every-other-Wednesday morning edition column written by a staff member who has been assigned the task will not do. There are superb education reporters and writers at work now, but their output has never reached the scale and credibility that are required.

Key professional associations need to accept the fact that the status quo is working neither for students nor for teachers and administrators and adjust their work accordingly. These associations are the National Association of Elementary School Principals, the National Association of Secondary School Principals, the Association for Supervision and Curriculum Development, and the American Association of School Administrators. In time, the larger, national groups must join: the National Education Association and the American Federation of Teachers.

These organizations have friends in Congress and in state legislatures, and their executive directors are familiar with which standing committees are likely to have sustained influence. The schools' lobbyists must argue for the existence and protection of a variety of schools, from the conservative to the progressive and everything in between. A variety of schools from among which parents and teachers can choose is valuable in a free democracy.

The line of their argument must include three foci:

First, we need a "core" curriculum that is flexibly imposed on all schools by state and federal governments. The core subjects identified by the late-nineteenth-century Committee of Ten on Secondary School Studies remain sensible: English, mathematics, science, history and the social sciences, and art. Beyond and within this core, each school should craft its own expression of these essential subjects, taking into account local wishes and traditions. If a community is relatively new—a district, say, that has been created as part of the breakup of an unwieldy jurisdiction—it must make the effort to explore what gives that community its special character.

Second, we must agree on what is adequate funding—adequate in the sense that there are ready mechanisms within a school's multiyear budgets to deal with inflation or deflation, ready in the sense that majorities of voters could be quickly gathered to cope with the pressures.

Third—and this is both a state and a federal matter—we must expand our use of the media. "Airtime" belongs to all of us; it is limited in breadth; no one entity should have absolute control of any sector. We must take back that part of the media that depends on state or nationally allocated slots in the communications spectrum, demanding that some of its powers be devoted to the task of education reform, within the schools and beyond them.

It is painful for a career educator such as me to admit that the flaws in our efforts are so great that they can no longer be ignored by the wider world. The way high schools currently work is familiar and thus congenial. I and other veterans like me know how to work within their boundaries, bringing small improvements to that sheltered space, such as changing the number of credits required for graduation (a largely meaningless exercise, similar to changing the ways that forks, knives, and spoons are set out on a formal dining table).

We insiders suffer from excessive optimism about our gigantic, decent, and, on the whole, well-intentioned enterprise. We believe that our efforts are as worthy as they are familiar and that they are enough. We even think that we deserve applause, so all too often we continue to stumble around. However, if we were to agree to take risks, what might lie ahead?

Public education should not be monolithic, and nonpublic education should be sensitive to the need for all sorts of secondary schools, ones demonstrably effective with many, if not all, adolescents. New kinds of schools and new kinds of "districts"—gatherings of schools that share beliefs, emphases, and designs—must be invented. There must be a variety among schools for parents or guardians to choose from, though this will be harder to provide in rural areas. I must ask myself whether, given my elder child's needs and interests, school A is likely to be better for her than school B. My younger child, in contrast, may flourish best in school B. Or even school C.

To assist parents in this important task, there must be transparency about each school. That is, any citizen should be able to find out as much about a school as a printed description might provide, and neutral authorities need to make such descriptions available. These descriptions must be widely available to every family of school-age children in a school district, and the central authorities must be sure that every parent of every school-age child has those descriptions, without exception. That is, schools should advertise themselves, in the best sense.

There must be advocacy by the government on behalf both of the discrete qualities of each school and of the fit of each school for each child's special interests, enthusiasms, and needs. There should be information sessions for families with school-age children and other local leaders provided on a regular basis, from town or city hall meetings to informal coffee parties.

The media, both public and for-profit outlets, must be required to set aside, at their expense, airtime at hours that best serve parents and children. Of course, just as there is not One Best system, there is also not One Best time for all parents and children; the media must be required to provide access to their offerings on a twenty-four-hour basis.

This approach will be messy, inevitably. Taking each potential student one by one and matching him or her with the school that appears to be most appropriate for him or her will take time and patience—the same kind of patience that one experiences in a medical clinic, waiting for the most appropriate health professional for each individual sickly child. All this represents a significant shift both in how formal schooling is structured and in how that new structure can best serve a population with varied needs. Comparison with medicine and the delivery of health-related services is apt.

Our task is the giving of an informed new shape to the ways that adolescents learn and thus the manner in which we teach them. Schooling is not merely a pedagogue's ritual created out of traditional ways, a dance that American citizens collectively experience. Instead, as professionals we take on the task of carrying out this moral duty to help each child, one by one, learn up to his or her greatest extent. Many of us may not be interested in putting our work in such an exalted frame. However, we cannot shirk that responsibility. It comes with our territory. We want our students to grow up to be informed, principled, and free.

Such lofty goals may appear mawkish to many of us. We do not want to overreach; as professionals we understandably hesitate to tamper too much with personal commitments and habits. As a school day ends with the familiar cacophony of lockers slamming and the jabbering of friends, the racket should give us hope, even confidence: these are not gods, but just ordinary people, and so are we. At the same time, these are deserving people, participants in our democracy, one person at a time.

Our work is worthy, essential to an orderly, optimistic democracy. Let us persist with it.

ACKNOWLEDGMENTS

This book was a joy to write for several reasons: it allowed me to review some ideas that had percolated in my mind for a good many months; it allowed me to relive some happy, or at least memorable, moments in the past years; and it reminded me how much I have depended on the love, depth, and imagination of my wife, Nancy.

The chapters that precede this note were written in the midst of my battle with colon cancer and its inevitable lifesaving, but debilitating, chemotherapy. Nancy keeps my spirits up, my hope for the future high, and my reasoning and syntax reasonably close to what a glinty-eyed history teacher (like her) would find acceptable.

My son-in-law, Jim Cullen, also helped me shape this book from a jumbled set of ideas into a readable text. Jim has several books to his credit and a PhD dissertation behind him, and is the History Department chair at the Fieldston School in New York City.

I also have appreciated the chance to talk about all my books over the years with good and interested friends, and for this one, especially with Sylvia Thayer, Philip Zaeder, and Art and Barbara Powell.

I am a lucky man.

FURTHER READING

Many readers will find this an odd list of texts for a book on high school reform. It is eclectic, I admit. But the fact remains that I did either read these books for the first time or "rediscover" them as I worked on my book's outline. However "off subject" they may at first appear, each kindled an idea or ideas that struck me as useful in making my argument. I cannot evade the responsibility to give credit where credit is due.

As you will find, many books and articles are woven into the script as it proceeded, and I have mentioned them there.

Mortimer J. Adler, *The Paideia Proposal: An Educational Manifesto* (New York: Macmillan, 1982).

Nicholas Baker, *Human Smoke: The Beginnings of World War II and the End of Civilization* (New York: Simon & Schuster, 2008).

Edward Banfield, *The Unheavenly City* (Prospect Heights, IL: Waveland Press, 1970).

Jane Brox, *Legacies of the American Farm* (New York: North Point Press, 2004).

Jim Cullen, *The Art of Democracy: A Concise History of Popular Culture in the United States*, 2nd ed. (Oxford: Blackwell, 2002).

Daedalus, the journal of the American Academy of Arts and Sciences, published by MIT Press. Published four times a year on a wide variety of subjects, save usually one each year focused on education, principally on higher education. I have found all the essays, on whatever topic, to be provocative.

William Damon, *The Path to Purpose: Helping Our Children Find Their Calling in Life* (New York: Free Press, 2008).

John Dewey, *Dewey on Education: Selections* (New York: Bureau of Publications, Teachers College, Columbia University). (There are dozens of collections of Dewey's work from a variety of publishers.) Always thoughtful even as written years ago.

Drew Gilpin Faust, *The Republic of Suffering: Death and the American Civil War* (New York: Knopf, 2008).

Chester E. Finn, *We Must Take Charge* (New York: Free Press, 1991).

Robert Frost, *Collected Poems* (found in a variety of editions by several publishers).

Howard Gardner, *The Disciplined Mind* (New York: Basic Books, 1991).

Jane Jacobs, *The Death and Life of Great American Cities* (New York: Random House, 1961).

Milbrey W. McLaughlin and Joan E. Talbert, *The Contexts of Teaching in Secondary Schools: Teachers' Realities* (New York: Columbia University Press, 1990).

Richard J. Murnane and Frank Levy, *Teaching the New Basic Skills: Principles for Educating Children to Thrive in a Changing Economy* (New York: Free Press, 1996).

David Perkins, *Smart Schools* (New York: Free Press, 1992).

Denise Clark Pope, *Doing School: How We Are Creating a Generation of Stressed Out, Materialistic, and Miseducated Students* (New Haven, CT: Yale University Press, 2001).

Arthur G. Powell, Eleanor Farrar, and David K. Cohen, *The Shopping Mall High School* (New York: Houghton Mifflin, 1985).

Nancy Faust Sizer, *Crossing the Stage: Redesigning Senior Year* (Portsmouth, NH: Heinemann, 2002).

Theodore R. Sizer and Nancy Faust Sizer, *The Students Are Watching: Schools and the Moral Contract* (Boston: Beacon Press, 1999).

ABOUT THE AUTHOR

Possibly because he was the youngest of six children, **Ted Sizer** was always a reformer. No matter how much delight and gratitude he took in his surroundings, he was always looking for a way to make them better. This was especially true of schools and of the classrooms inside them. And no matter how much of a rush he was in, he always knew that he needed colleagues, not only for the ideas they gave him but also for the lasting effect that working together would bring to their projects and plans. An essentially modest man, he was not looking to be a hero, but his plans were grand ones. He wanted no less than to help build a movement.

After earning a BA at Yale and a PhD at Harvard, and after leading two venerable educational institutions—the Harvard Graduate School of Education and Phillips Academy in Andover—he went on to found a new institution, the Coalition of Essential Schools (CES). He called CES a "Conversation Among Friends." Their "bible" was a collection of principles in which they believed. All the other particularities involved in school keeping—the vast number of beliefs and practices that come into every day's work—were to be decided by those who understood the context and knew the students. His conviction was that there were to be no rules, not even models, but that the collaboration of people from different schools would act as an inspiration and a support.

His writing then became even more important to him, as he knew that his travels, relationships, experiences, and observations might well facilitate the work of those who worked within schools. The first book in his Horace series was a critique, but he followed it with five more books that described the best work he saw in school reform. Teachers were described in detail, often in what he called "fiction/nonfiction," and from those portraits other teachers took heart. His teaching at Brown University, where CES was based, and later at the Harvard Graduate School of Education was also very important to him, because it too served as a way to draw brilliant, energetic, and brave reformers into this important national effort.

I said to the CES Fall Forum a year after his death that I hoped that the teachers there, even if they had never met Ted Sizer, would consider themselves his valued colleagues. This book continues that connection.

Nancy Faust Sizer

INDEX